Essex

WALKS

Compiled by
Brian Conduit

Acknowledgements
My thanks for the valuable advice and numerous leaflets that
I obtained from the various tourist information centres
throughout the area. *The Essex Directory of Walks and Rides*,
produced by the county council, was particularly useful.

Text:	Brian Conduit
Photography:	Brian Conduit and Jarrold Publishing
Editor:	Geoffrey Sutton
Designers:	Doug Whitworth
Mapping:	Heather Pearson

Series Consultant:	Brian Conduit

Jarrold Publishing   ISBN 0-7117-0551-8

While every care has been taken to ensure the accuracy
of the route directions, the publishers cannot accept
responsibility for errors or omissions, or for changes in
details given. The countryside is not static: hedges and
fences can be removed, field boundaries can be altered,
footpaths can be rerouted and changes in ownership can
result in the closure or diversion of some concessionary
paths. Also, paths that are easy and pleasant for walking
in fine conditions may become slippery, muddy and
difficult in wet weather, while stepping-stones across
rivers and streams may become impassable.

If you find an inaccuracy in either the text or maps,
please write to or e-mail Jarrold Publishing at the
addresses below.

First published 2001
by Jarrold Publishing

Printed in Belgium
by Proost NV, Turnhout. 1/01

Jarrold Publishing
Pathfinder Guides, Whitefriars, Norwich NR3 1TR
E-mail: pathfinder@jarrold.com
www.jarrold-publishing.co.uk/pathfinders

Front cover: An Essex woodland scene
Previous page: Hedingham Castle

Contents

Short, easy walks

Walks of modest
length, likely to
involve some
modest uphill
walking

More challenging
walks which may
be longer and/or
over more rugged
terrain, often with
some stiff climbs

Keymap

SCALE 1:384 615 or 1 INCH to about 6 MILES *1CM to 3.8KM*

KEYMAP HEIGHTS SHOWN IN FEET

Keymap

At-a-glance...

Walk	Page	Start	Nat. Grid Reference	Distance	Time
Audley Park and Wendens Ambo	66	Saffron Waldon	TL 539385	7$\frac{1}{2}$ miles (12.1km)	3$\frac{1}{2}$ hrs
Benfleet Downs and Hadleigh Marsh	51	Hadleigh Castle Country Park, Chapel Lane car park	TQ 799869	6$\frac{1}{2}$ miles (10.5km)	3 hrs
Burnham and the River Crouch	72	Burnham-on-Crouch	TR 951956	8$\frac{1}{2}$ miles (13.7km)	4 hrs
Castle Hedingham and the River Colne	48	Castle Hedingham	TL 785355	6 miles (9.7km)	3 hrs
Chipping Ongar and Greensted church	22	Chipping Ongar	TL 552032	4$\frac{1}{2}$ miles (7.2km)	2$\frac{1}{2}$ hrs
Coggeshall and Feering	57	Coggeshall	TL 850223	7$\frac{1}{2}$ miles (12.1km)	4 hrs
Epping Forest and Upshire	82	High Beach, Epping Forest Centre	TL 413981	9 miles (14.5km)	4$\frac{1}{2}$ hrs
Finchingfield and Great Bardfield	29	Finchingfield	TL 685328	5 miles (8km)	2$\frac{1}{2}$ hrs
Great Dunmow and Little Easton	42	Great Dunmow	TL 627220	5$\frac{1}{2}$ miles (8.9km)	2$\frac{1}{2}$ hrs
Hanningfield Reservoir	20	Hanningfield Reservoir	TQ 737976	4 miles (6.4km)	2 hrs
Hatfield Forest	38	Hatfield Forest	TL 547203	5$\frac{1}{2}$ miles (8.9km)	2$\frac{1}{2}$ hrs
High Woods and Colchester	26	High Woods Country Park	TL 999271	4$\frac{1}{2}$ miles (7.2km)	2 hrs
Ingatestone and Mountnessing	69	Ingatestone	TQ 651996	8$\frac{1}{2}$ miles (13.7km)	4$\frac{1}{2}$ hrs
Laindon Common and the Bursteads	14	Laindon Common (A176)	TQ 674930	3 miles (4.8km)	1$\frac{1}{2}$ hrs
Maldon and the Blackwater estuary	75	Maldon, Promenade Park	TL 863065	9 miles (14.5km)	4$\frac{1}{2}$ hrs
Mersea Island	32	Cudmore Grove Country Park	TM 065146	5$\frac{1}{2}$ miles (8.9km)	2$\frac{1}{2}$ hrs
Mill Green and Blackmore	54	Millgreen Common	TL 638013	6$\frac{1}{2}$ miles (10.5km)	3$\frac{1}{2}$ hrs
The Naze and Walton Channel	18	The Naze car park	TM 265234	4 miles (6.4km)	2 hrs
Newport and Debden	60	Newport Station car park	TL 522335	6$\frac{1}{2}$ miles (10.5km)	3$\frac{1}{2}$ hrs
Pleshey and Great Waltham	36	Pleshey	Tl 664144	5$\frac{1}{2}$ miles (8.9km)	2$\frac{1}{2}$ hrs
St Osyth Creek	40	St Osyth	TM 122155	6 miles (9.7km)	3 hrs
St Peter's Chapel, Bradwell Marshes and Tillingham	86	Bradwell Marina, Bradwell Waterside	TM 994077	11 miles (17.5km)	5 hrs
Stour valley: Constable Country	63	Manningtree Station	TM 094322	7$\frac{1}{2}$ miles (12.1km)	4 hrs
Thaxted	45	Thaxted	TL 612310	6$\frac{1}{2}$ miles (10.5km)	3 hrs
Thorndon Country Park	24	Thorndon Country Park North	TQ 606915	4$\frac{1}{2}$ miles (7.2km)	2$\frac{1}{2}$ hrs
Waltham Abbey and the Lee valley	16	Waltham Abbey, Lee Valley Park Info. Centre	TL 384007	4$\frac{1}{2}$ miles (7.2km)	2 hrs
Weald Country Park	34	Weald Country Park, Visitor Centre car park	TQ 568942	5 miles (8km)	2$\frac{1}{2}$ hrs
White Notley and Cressing	78	Cressing Station	TL 776203	9$\frac{1}{2}$ miles (15.3km)	5 hrs

Comments

Apart from the attractions of Saffron Walden, the route includes parkland, views of a great house and a picturesque village and church.

The walk includes grassland, woodland and marsh, and there are grand views across the Thames estuary. You can also visit a ruined medieval castle painted by Constable.

Much of the walk is beside the River Crouch and there are fine and unimpeded views across the surrounding marshland and meadowland.

There are fine views over the Colne valley, a picturesque village and the chance to visit a magnificent Norman castle.

The walk takes you through some of the pleasant and open countryside near Chipping Ongar and passes the unique wooden Saxon church at Greensted.

Coggeshall is one of the most appealing towns in Essex and there is plenty of historic interest on this walk in the valley of the River Blackwater.

Apart from an incursion into open country near Upshire, the whole of this walk is through the superb woodlands of Epping Forest.

The walk takes in two exceptionally attractive villages and much pleasant countryside in between.

Great Dunmow is an attractive town, Little Easton has a fine church, and the walk uses a mixture of disused railway track, field paths and riverside meadows.

From several points on the walk there are fine views of Hanningfield Reservoir and across the Thames estuary to the line of the North Downs.

This easy walk in Hatfield Forest takes you through what is probably the finest surviving example of an authentic medieval forest landscape.

From a country park based on a fragment of medieval forest, the route takes you into Colchester for a walk around some of its historic sites, through parkland and beside the River Colne.

Two halls, three churches, a windmill and extensive views over the surrounding countryside are the main ingredients of this lengthy but undemanding walk.

A short and easy walk which starts at a surviving area of common and takes in the churches at Great Burstead and Little Burstead.

This pleasant and varied walk is almost entirely beside water and gives you the opportunity to explore the attractive old town of Maldon.

From this walk at the eastern tip of Mersea Island, there are extensive views both over the island and across the water to the Essex mainland.

The walk includes woodland and common, remnants of an ancient forest, and passes through the attractive village of Blackmore.

After walking along the cliffs of the Naze, the route turns inland and keeps along the top of an embankment, above marshes, creeks and channels, through a nature reserve.

There are fine views, both Newport and Debden are attractive villages and the route passes through parkland on the return leg.

The walk takes you through the valley of Walthambury Brook between Pleshey and Great Waltham. There is the motte of a Norman castle and defensive earthworks to see at Pleshey.

Starting from a superb monastic gatehouse, this is a walk of wide and extensive views amongst the creeks and marshes of the Colne estuary.

This lengthy and exhilarating walk across the lonely and desolate marshes of the Dengie peninsula takes in three villages, two churches and a remote Saxon chapel.

This is the classic Constable Country walk on the Essex-Suffolk border that takes you through Dedham and the beautiful Dedham Vale, passing Flatford Mill and Willy Lott's Cottage.

The small medieval town of Thaxted, dominated by its magnificent church, is the focal point of this walk in the upper Chelmer valley.

The attractive woodlands of a country park are combined with open countryside and views across the Thames estuary.

Starting from an impressive Norman abbey – the alleged burial place of King Harold – the walk explores the meadows, wetlands and waterways of the Lee Valley Park.

Weald Country Park provides pleasant and easy walking through woodlands, across grassland and beside a lake.

Villages, old churches and the interesting Cressing Temple are among the attractions of this walk in the pleasant landscape of the Brain valley.

At-a-glance...

Introduction
to Essex

Although not at first glance an obvious magnet for walkers – lacking the dramatic appeal of hill-walking country – Essex does possess much fine and varied countryside. Its great expanses of lonely marshes, rolling farmlands, ancient woodlands, wide views and attractive towns and villages, more than compensate for the lack of high hills, extensive moorlands and a rugged coastline.

Unspoilt countryside

The county tends to suffer from several misconceptions and wild generalisations and three of the commonest of these – held it must be said only by those whose knowledge of Essex is fairly limited – is that it is flat, over-crowded and uninteresting.

It cannot be denied that there is a lot of flat country in Essex – as there is indeed in many other counties – but in general the landscape is best described as gently undulating. The hilliest country is in the north and west, near the Hertfordshire and Cambridgeshire borders. The county certainly suffers from the same population and traffic pressures as the other Home Counties, and many of its towns and villages have experienced substantial growth in the last two decades, but there is still plenty of open, unspoilt and tranquil countryside, especially further away from London you get.

On the marshes of the Essex coast there is a genuine feeling of solitude and remoteness that is hard to find anywhere else in southern England. And by no stretch of the imagination can any county be dismissed as uninteresting when it possesses the oldest recorded town in Britain, some outstandingly attractive and distinctive villages and small towns, some superb medieval churches and a wealth of historic buildings, as well as much pleasant scenery and some of the finest surviving fragments of England's medieval forests.

Undulating farmland, coastal views and ancient woodland

Essex spreads northwards from the Thames estuary to the borders of Suffolk and Cambridgeshire and eastwards from London and Hertfordshire to the North Sea coast. The coast is mainly flat, marshy and heavily indented, separated into peninsulas by broad estuaries. On the south the Thames estuary divides the county from Kent and on the north the Stour estuary is its border with Suffolk. In between are the estuaries of the Crouch, Blackwater and Colne. The extensive marshes, creeks and mudflats provide a haunting and strangely beautiful landscape of wide and

Willy Lott's Cottage at Flatford, just over the border in Suffolk

unimpeded vistas. Only in the north – at The Naze – are there cliffs and these are continually crumbling away under the onslaught of North Sea gales.

Inland the landscape is undulating and well-wooded, containing much good, fertile farmland. In the Middle Ages a large proportion of the county comprised the Forest of Essex, a vast royal hunting-ground covered by dense woodland and rough heath, protected for the royal sport by a draconian code of laws. For those who infringed the forest laws punishments were severe: execution or mutilation for major offences, like killing one of the royal beasts, and fines of imprisonment for lesser crimes, such as the unauthorised felling of trees.

Over the centuries these laws lapsed and became redundant and the forest decreased in area as the mighty trees were felled and the land became converted to agricultural uses. Now only fragments remain but some of these are quite sizeable, making Essex still one of the most wooded of English counties. Most extensive and popular of these fragments is Epping Forest, a thin but long wedge of ancient woodland, covering nearly 6,000 acres (2,428 ha) and stretching northwards from London's East End to Epping. It is a vital open space noted for its grassy plains and its superb woodlands of hornbeam, oak, beech and birch. The forest only survived further destruction as a result of prompt action by the Corporation of the City of London, which took it over by Act of Parliament in 1878 and subsequently conserved it as a recreational amenity.

Other surviving forests are Hainault, near Chigwell, bought by London

In the Weald Country Park, north-west of Brentwood

County Council in 1903 and later made into a country park, and Hatfield, near Bishop's Stortford, a National Trust property. There are smaller remnants of the forests of Writtle (near Chelmsford) and Kingswood (near Colchester), plus numerous woodlands.

On the northern fringes of Essex, near the boundaries with Cambridgeshire and Suffolk, the landscape is hillier and less wooded. This is sheep-farming country, and in the later Middle Ages this part of the county shared – along with neighbouring Suffolk – in the flourishing East Anglian woollen industry and cloth trade. This is evident in some of the small towns and villages where handsome old buildings are presided over by lofty and spacious 15th-century 'wool churches' – echoing the well-known wool churches of the Cotswolds – all built from the profits of the cloth trade. Three of the grandest of these churches are to be found at Saffron Walden, Thaxted and Dedham.

Wooden churches, estuary ports and pretty villages
In complete contrast to these magnificent wool churches, the churches in the former forested – and thus poorer – parts of the county are much smaller and plainer, often with simple wooden bell-turrets instead of towers and spires. These churches are amongst the most charming and distinctive features of the Essex landscape. Of particular interest and appeal is the unique timber church at Greensted, near Chipping Ongar, which dates from the Saxon period.

The woollen towns of Thaxted, Dedham and Saffron Walden are among the most attractive in the county. Two others are the estuary ports of Maldon and Burnham-on-Crouch, both of which have interesting quaysides and a number of fine buildings. Pretty villages are too numerous to mention but particular mention must be made of Finchingfield, a classic English village with its combination of duck pond and old cottages presided over by a medieval church.

From Camulodunum to Audley End

It was the Saxons who gave their name to Essex but its history goes back much further. Before the Roman invasion, Camulodunum (Colchester) was a major tribal capital, referred to by the Roman writer Pliny in AD 77. This is the earliest reference to any settlement in the country and Colchester can therefore claim to be Britain's oldest recorded town. After its capture it was rebuilt by the Romans as a legionary fortress and was their base for the conquest of Britain. During Boudicca's rebellion in AD 60, it was sacked and burnt and had to be rebuilt, this time as a civilian settlement. Colchester still retains much of its Roman walls and possesses one of only two surviving Roman gateways in the country. A whole day could be spent wandering around this fascinating city.

After the withdrawal of the Romans, Saxon invaders penetrated the area, moving from the coast up the estuaries and on through the river valleys, to create the Kingdom of the East Saxons or Essex. Viking invaders followed, and after 1066 the Normans quickly established themselves in the area. William the Conqueror built the largest keep in England at Colchester, on the site of the Roman temple, still an most impressive sight and now housing an extensive museum. Other outstanding medieval castles are at

The outstanding medieval timbered barns at Cressing Temple

St Osyth Priory

Castle Hedingham and Hadleigh, with lesser remains at Saffron Walden and Pleshey.

Essex has other associations with the Norman Conquest. At Waltham Abbey is the alleged grave of King Harold, whose body was brought here after his defeat at Hastings. The 12th-century nave of the abbey is undoubtedly the most imposing of the county's monastic remains. Others include the ruins of St Botolph's Priory in the centre of Colchester, built partly – as was much of the rest of the town – from recycled Roman bricks, and the ornate, late medieval gatehouse of St Osyth Priory, one of the finest of such structures in the country.

In the post-medieval period, as the forest was progressively cleared, conditions became more settled and agriculture prospered, a number of great country-houses were built. The most impressive of these is the great 17th-century palace of the earls of Suffolk at Audley End, set in acres of attractive parkland on the edge of Saffron Walden.

John Constable, the seaside and forest recreation

One man who did more than most to put Essex on the map was John Constable, England's most famous landscape painter, although the county has to share him with neighbouring Suffolk. 'Constable Country', where the artist was born, lived and worked, is around Dedham Vale in the Stour valley, and thousands are attracted to this area on the Essex-Suffolk border to see the landscapes that inspired his best-known works and visit the buildings he painted.

In the Victorian railway era, a combination of sandy beaches and proximity to the capital led to the rapid growth of seaside resorts along the Essex coast at Southend, Clacton, Walton-on-the-Naze and elsewhere. Even more convenient for

Audley End

Londoners was Epping Forest, and regular excursions to the forest and holidays on the Essex coast became a part of the way of life for many people in London and the Home Counties.

Recently Essex has become a commuter belt and a centre for new 'hi-tech' industries, and there has been a tremendous growth of population, especially in the west of the county. But despite these pressures, a perhaps surprisingly large amount of the older and quieter Essex survives amidst the modern bustle.

Approaching Thaxted

Walking in Essex

Essex is obviously not for those who want dramatic landscapes or rugged hill and moorland walking. After all the highest point in the county, just outside the village of Langley – in the far north-west near the Hertfordshire and Cambridgeshire borders – only rises to 482ft (147m). But there is more to walking than long hikes and exhausting climbs over challenging terrain, and Essex retains plenty of pleasant and unspoilt countryside, enhanced by attractive old towns, pretty villages and interesting historic monuments.

Given the nature of the terrain, the orange-coded walks in this guide – numbers 23 to 28 – are all placed in that category because of their length not because there is anything strenuous about them. Waymarking is generally good and there is an abundance of long-distance routes – Forest Way, Three Forests Way, Essex Way, St Peter's Way, Stour Valley Path, Harcamlow Way – which snake across the county and provide generally trouble-free route finding. The likeliest hazards – common to all arable areas – are that some of the narrow field-edge and enclosed paths can become muddy in winter or after rain, and in high summer sometimes get overgrown with nettles and brambles, a relatively small price to pay for a good walk.

Laindon Common and the Bursteads

Start	Laindon Common, at junction of A176 and lane to Little Burstead about 1 mile (1.6km) south of Billericay
Distance	3 miles (4.8km)
Approximate time	1½ hours
Parking	Laindon Common
Refreshments	Pub at Laindon Common
Ordnance Survey maps	Landranger 177 (East London, Billericay & Gravesend), Explorer 175 (Southend-on-Sea & Basildon)

This short walk takes you through an area of open and pleasant countryside between Billericay and Basildon, passing the church at Great Burstead and the smaller isolated church at Little Burstead. The final stretch is across the wooded Laindon Common. Some of the field paths may be muddy and overgrown at certain times of the year.

Turn right out of the car park – not along the road but along the parallel drive – to the A176, cross carefully and, at a public footpath sign, turn right through a kissing-gate. Walk along an enclosed path, continue along a track

Great Burstead

by farm buildings and then keep along the right-hand edge of a field.

In the field corner continue along a narrow enclosed path – the tower and spire of Great Burstead church come into view – which emerges via a stile on to a road **A**. The medieval church is to the left but the route continues to the

right to a T-junction. Turn left, almost immediately turn right, at a public footpath sign to Little Burstead church, along a drive and continue along an enclosed path (between garden fences) which descends gently through trees to a footbridge over a brook. Cross it, head up an embankment to enter a field and continue across it, going over a slight brow and making for a waymarked post on the far side.

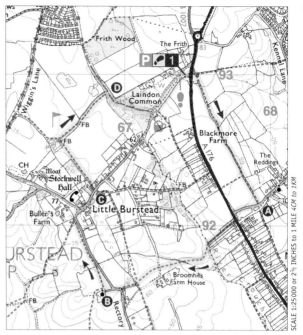

Cross a plank footbridge and keep in the same direction across the next field towards a hedge corner. Continue parallel to the left-hand edge of this field and the next one and bear slightly right to a waymarked post on the far side. Keep ahead over a plank foot-bridge and through a hedge gap and then walk along the left-hand field edge, looking out for where you bear left through a hedge gap on to a road. Turn right and, where the road bends right, keep ahead along a track to Little Burstead church.

This delightful small church has a Norman nave and the usual Essex 15th-century wooden belfry.

Immediately on entering the church-yard, turn right **B** over a stile and walk across a field, making for the start of a hedge-line on the right-hand edge. Continue by the hedge, parallel to a road, climb a stile in the field corner and keep ahead along the road through Little Burstead. At a public footpath sign to Wiggins Lane and Laindon Common, turn left **C** along a narrow enclosed path which bends first right and then left to reach a barrier.

Pass beside it, walk along the left-

hand edge of Burstead golf course and at a hedge corner on the left, keep straight ahead to pick up and continue along the left-hand edge again. Climb a stile, cross a plank footbridge to reach a track and turn right to continue across the golf course, by a hedge on the right. Look out for where you turn right to cross a footbridge and turn left, now with the hedge on the left. In the field corner go through a kissing-gate, cross a footbridge and turn right **D** along a path through the woodland of Laindon Common.

Look out for where a path leads off to the left – there is a Basildon District Circular Footpath post here – to join another path, turn right along it and the path emerges on to a road opposite the Burstead Village Inn. Even if you miss the path to the left, you will end up in the same place opposite the pub. Cross the road and turn left along a path through trees – parallel to the road – which leads back to the start. ●

Waltham Abbey and the Lee valley

Start	Waltham Abbey, Lee Valley Park Information Centre
Distance	4½ miles (7.2km)
Approximate time	2 hours
Parking	Lee Valley Park Information Centre
Refreshments	Pubs and cafés at Waltham Abbey
Ordnance Survey maps	Landranger 166 (Luton & Hertford), Explorer 174 (Epping Forest & Lee Valley)

The walk takes you through part of the Lee Valley Park just to the north of Waltham Abbey, an area of grassland, marsh, lakes and waterways, largely reclaimed from gravel extraction and once the site of gunpowder works. There are attractive views across riverside meadows and most of the route is beside water. Historic interest is centred on the fine Norman abbey at the start.

Start at the information centre and, facing the abbey, turn right to pass under the 14th-century abbey gateway and turn left beside Cornmill Stream. Cross a footbridge and keep ahead into the town, passing in front of the abbey.

Apart from the early 12th-century nave of an earlier church – an outstanding example of Norman architecture – little else remains of the great and wealthy Augustinian abbey founded in 1177 by Henry II as part of his penance for the murder of Thomas Becket. The unfortunate King Harold is supposed to have been buried behind the high altar after his defeat and death at the Battle of Hastings in 1066, and the site of his alleged tomb can be seen to the east of the church. The abbey was dissolved by Henry VIII in 1540.

Turn right along Highbridge Street, keep ahead in the Waltham Cross direction to cross High Bridge over the Horsemill Stream and after crossing a second channel – the River Lee Navigation – turn right **A** at a public footpath sign, to join the towpath beside it. As you walk along, it is difficult to envisage this now green and tranquil area as once being the site of a gunpowder factory.

Continue along the towpath – passing by two locks and under a bridge – as far as a fingerpost in front of the second bridge. Bear left here off the towpath, turn sharp right **B** to cross the bridge and walk along a tarmac path, between pools and marshland. Continue through trees and cross a footbridge to reach Hooks Marsh car park. Keep ahead over the Horsemill Stream and along a tarmac drive. Just after passing Fishers Green Farm, turn right over a stile **C**. Continue along the right-hand edge of a field and, at a footpath post, turn left, in the Cornmill Meadow direction, and walk across a field to a track by the corner of

a high wire fence.

Bear right to cross the track, keep along the right-hand field edge beside the high fence and go through a kissing-gate in the field corner. Continue along the right-hand edge of a meadow, follow the fence round to the right, and the path bears first right and then left to reach a footbridge over Cornmill Stream. Turn right over it, turn left **D** to walk along a most attractive path beside the stream, and soon the tower of Waltham Abbey can be seen across the meadows to the right.

Go through a kissing-gate and continue by the stream, curving gradually right towards the abbey. At the far end of the meadow, go through another kissing-gate and turn first right and then left to follow the path under a road. After crossing a footbridge into the Abbey Grounds, keep ahead to the start.

Waltham Abbey

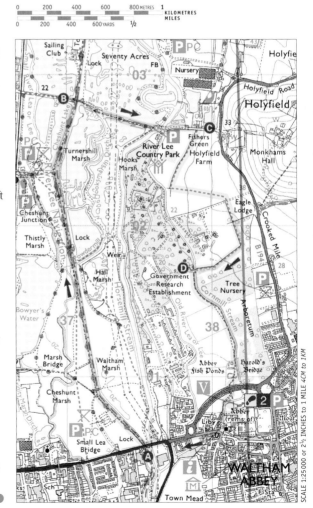

The Naze and Walton Channel

Start	The Naze car park, 1½ miles (2.4km) north of Walton-on-the-Naze
Distance	4 miles (6.4km)
Approximate time	2 hours
Parking	The Naze
Refreshments	Beach café (seasonal) at The Naze
Ordnance Survey maps	Landranger 169 (Ipswich & The Naze, Clacton- on-Sea), Explorer 184 (Colchester, Harwich & Clacton-on-Sea)

Starting by The Naze Tower, the first part of this exhilarating walk of wide vistas is along the cliffs of The Naze. You then turn away from the sea and continue along the top of an embankment above creeks, marshes, mudflats and inlets to the edge of the small resort of Walton-on-the-Naze. A final short stretch – along a road and then the coast path – brings you back to the start. Much of the route is through a nature reserve and is ideal for observing both shipping and wildlife.

The word 'naze' comes from an old English for 'nose' and refers to the original shape of the headland. The high but crumbly cliffs – constantly being eaten away by the sea – are a rarity on the generally flat Essex coast.

Begin by heading across to The Naze Tower, built in 1720 by Trinity House as a landmark, and continue northwards across the grassy clifftop, heeding the

Creeks near The Naze

warning notices to keep well clear of the unstable edge. As the path descends to keep across the top of lower cliffs, Harwich can be seen ahead.

At one point a slight detour has to be made to the left between gorse bushes to a T-junction. Turn right, turn right again at a crossroads and immediately turn left to continue along the coast path. On joining a tarmac path, bear left **A** on to it to walk on top of an embankment, above pools and marshes and along the edge of an Essex Wildlife Trust nature reserve. Where this tarmac path ends, bear left again to continue along a pleasant grassy path – still on the top of an embankment – above Cormorant Creek and the surrounding marshland. The Naze Tower stands out prominently on the skyline to the left.

The path bends sharp left **B** to keep by the broader expanses of Walton Channel on the right and above Walton Hall Marshes on the left. A few yards before reaching a track in front of a caravan park, turn left and climb a stile above a small pool on the right. Keep ahead to climb another one, and the path bends right to emerge on to a road on the edge of Walton-on-the-Naze **C**.

Turn left gently uphill and where the road bears left – by a sign for The Naze – bear right on to a track and then bear left on to a narrow enclosed path. At the top of steps, turn left to a track and turn right along it to return to the starting point. ●

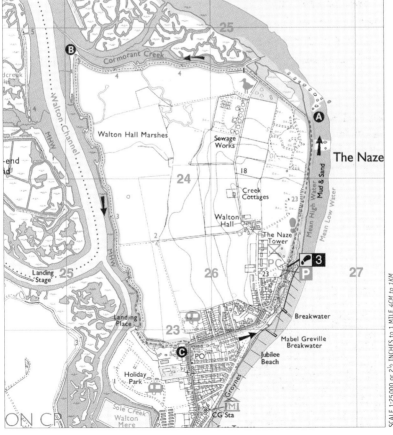

Hanningfield Reservoir

Start	Hanningfield Reservoir, signposted from A130 to the south of Chelmsford
Distance	4 miles (6.4km)
Approximate time	2 hours
Parking	Hanningfield Reservoir
Refreshments	Café at start, pub at South Hanningfield
Ordnance Survey maps	Landranger 167 (Chelmsford, Harlow & Bishop's Stortford), Explorer 175 (Southend- on-Sea & Basildon)

The fine views over Hanningfield Reservoir – at the start and near the end of the walk – are especially welcome in an area lacking in natural lakes. In clear conditions there are also extensive views looking southwards across the Thames estuary to the line of the North Downs on the horizon. Hanningfield Reservoir was constructed in the 1950s and is now a Site of Special Scientific Interest, renowned for its wildfowl. It is also popular for fishing and sailing.

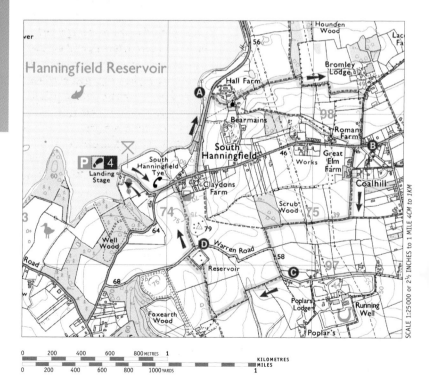

SCALE 1:25000 or 2½ INCHES to 1 MILE 4CM to 1KM

Start by walking away from the reservoir along the drive to the road and turn left into South Hanningfield. Turn left along the road to West Hanningfield and, at a public footpath sign, turn right over a stile Ⓐ.

Walk along the left-hand edge of a field towards South Hanningfield church. The nave is Norman, the belfry was added in the 15th century and the east end was largely rebuilt in the 19th century.

Bear right, away from the field edge, to go through a kissing-gate, pass to the right of the church and turn left along the right-hand edge of the churchyard to a stile in the corner. Climb it, keep along the right-hand edge of the next two fields and, in the corner of the second one, climb two stiles in quick succession and cross a plank footbridge. Turn right along the right-hand edge of the next field, follow the edge round to the left and climb a stile. Again turn right along the right-hand field edge, follow the edge to the left and in the far corner cross a plank footbridge and climb two stiles in quick succession.

Walk across the next field, negotiate another double stile and an intervening plank footbridge and turn right along a hedge-lined track to a road Ⓑ. Turn right and, at a public footpath sign, turn left along the tarmac drive to Great Elms Farm. Where the drive turns right into the farmyard, climb the stile in front, keep ahead to cross a plank footbridge and climb a stile into a field. Walk along the right-hand field edge, negotiate a fence and keep ahead to climb a stile in the field corner to a T-junction. Turn right along an enclosed track, continue along the left-hand edge of a field, bear left through a hedge gap in the corner and walk along the right-hand edge of the next field alongside Scrub Wood. Do not climb the stile in the field corner but turn left to

Hanningfield Reservoir

continue along the right-hand field edge and climb a stile on to a lane. Keep ahead and just before a left bend, turn right Ⓒ through a gap beside a gate, and a waymarked post points the way along the right-hand edge of a field. From here there are fine and extensive views to the left, looking across the Thames estuary to the North Downs.

Continue downhill along the right-hand edge of the next field, turn right over a plank footbridge in the corner, turn left along the left-hand edge of the next field and pass through a hedge gap. Turn left along the left-hand field edge, follow the edge to the right and, in the next corner, turn right along the left-hand field edge. Almost immediately bear left through a hedge gap, continue uphill along the right-hand edge of a field and, in the corner, turn right through another hedge gap.

Turn left, keep ahead towards a reservoir embankment, continue below it, beside a high wire fence, and climb a stile on to a lane. Turn right, turn left Ⓓ over a stile, at a public footpath sign, and walk along the right-hand edge of a field. Continue along a path that bears right to a waymarked post and turn left gently downhill. Ahead is a superb view over Hanningfield Reservoir. In the bottom field corner, follow the path first to the left and then to the right to emerge into the car park of the Old Windmill pub. Keep ahead to the road and turn left to retrace your steps to the start. ●

Chipping Ongar and Greensted church

Start	Chipping Ongar
Distance	4½ miles (7.2km)
Approximate time	2½ hours
Parking	Chipping Ongar
Refreshments	Pubs and cafés at Chipping Ongar
Ordnance Survey maps	Landranger 167 (Chelmsford, Harlow & Bishop's Stortford), Explorer 183 (Chelmsford & The Rodings)

After passing by the moat and earthworks of the largely vanished castle at Chipping Ongar, this well-waymarked route takes you across the gently undulating countryside of the Roding valley to the famous wooden church at Greensted. From there an easy stroll along the Essex Way leads back to the start.

The walk starts in the centre of the pleasant and ancient market town of Chipping Ongar by the library and Budworth Hall, the latter a Victorian building with a clock tower erected to commemorate Queen Victoria's Golden Jubilee in 1887. Walk through the car park to the left of the library and, at a footpath sign to Ongar Castle, keep along the path ahead beside the castle moat to a kissing-gate. Only the mound or motte remains of the Norman castle.

Go through the kissing-gate, bear right along the right-hand field edge, go through another kissing-gate on to a track and turn right. The track curves left but you immediately bear right along a winding, fence-lined path beside the castle moat again to emerge on to a lane. Keep ahead downhill to the bottom end of the main street, passing to the left of the church. Apart from the 15th-century steeple and 19th-century south aisle and west porch, the church is still basically the original Norman

structure built around 1080.

Turn left and, just after crossing a bridge over the River Roding, turn right **A** in the Greensted and Toot Hill direction. Where the road bends right, keep ahead along a tarmac path and cross a drive to a stile. Climb it, walk along the left-hand edge of two fields and then continue along an enclosed path. The path bears left to pass between two pools and on through a belt of trees and bushes to enter a field. Turn right to continue along the right-hand edge, which curves left, and look out for where a waymarked post directs you to turn right through a hedge gap. Turn left, walk along the left-hand edge of two fields and go through a hedge gap on to a lane **B**.

Turn left and after about 20 yds (18m) turn right on to a path through a belt of trees and continue along the right-hand edge of a field. At a way-marked post, just before reaching a farm, turn right over a stile – here

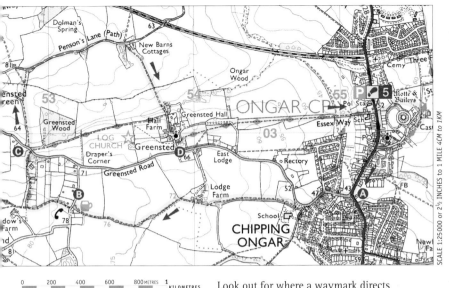

SCALE 1:25 000 or 2½ INCHES to 1 MILE 4CM to 1KM

0	200	400	600	800 METRES	**1**		KILOMETRES
							MILES
0	200	400	600 YARDS		½		

joining the Essex Way – and continue along the left-hand edge of a succession of fields and over a series of stiles. After the last field, keep ahead between trees, bear left to climb a stile and turn right along the right-hand edge of a field, heading gently downhill to a road.

Turn left and, at a public footpath sign to Penson's Lane, turn right **C** over a footbridge and head gently uphill along a left-hand field edge, by a new plantation on the right. At a way-marked post, pass through a fence gap to a fork and take the right-hand enclosed path. Cross a footbridge and climb a stile, continue along the right-hand edge of the next field, climb another stile and keep ahead through trees and over a plank footbridge to a T-junction. Turn right and walk along an attractive, tree-lined path (Penson's Lane) as far as a footpath post where you turn right through trees to a stile.

Climb the stile and bear left along the left-hand field edge, following the edge to the right. Continue gently downhill between fields. At the bottom follow the track around left and right bends and head gently uphill towards farm buildings.

Look out for where a waymark directs you up steps and through a gate and keep ahead along a gravel track to emerge on a lane by Greensted church.

This delightful little Saxon church is of unique interest as the only remaining wooden church in England and indeed it claims to be the oldest wooden church in the world. It was built around 1060, and the wooden walls of the nave survive from the original Saxon structure. Over the centuries the church has been enlarged and restored several times; the chancel was rebuilt in brick around 1500, and the timber tower and shingle spire – complete with traditional Essex weatherboard cladding – probably date from the early 17th century.

Turn left **D** along a tarmac track, at a public footpath sign to Ongar, and where the track bears left, keep ahead through a gate and follow a grassy path across a field to a gate in the far left-hand corner. Go through, bear left to continue along the left-hand edge of the next field, go through a kissing-gate, cross a track and keep ahead to a stile.

Climb it and keep in a straight line across fields towards Chipping Ongar. Finally cross a bridge over the river and head uphill along a track to the start. ●

CHIPPING ONGAR AND GREENSTED CHURCH ● **23**

Thorndon Country Park

Start	Thorndon Country Park North, signposted from A128 to south of Brentwood
Distance	4½ miles (7.2km)
Approximate time	2½ hours
Parking	Thorndon Country Park North
Refreshments	Light refreshments at Thorndon Country Centre
Ordnance Survey maps	Landranger 177 (East London, Billericay & Gravesend), Explorer 175 (Southend-on-Sea & Basildon)

The route uses a combination of public footpaths, waymarked trails and courtesy paths to create a most attractive and varied circuit of Thorndon Country Park, once part of the large estate surrounding Thorndon Hall. There are pools, meadows, some superb woodlands, parkland and grand views looking across the Thames estuary to the line of the North Downs in Kent.

The walk starts by the Countryside Centre where there is a display area and gift shop. It was built from trees that were felled in the 1987 hurricane. With your back to the Centre, turn right along a path into woodland, signposted Woodland Trail. Continue along this red-waymarked route by turning right in front of a large tree but, at the next waymarked post, turn left off the Woodland Trail and head across to

In Thorndon Country Park

climb steps into a car park.

Walk across the car park, descend steps on the far side and continue along the path ahead, crossing a plank footbridge and continuing to a tarmac drive **A**. Cross the drive and at a fork take the right-hand path (public footpath sign to Herongate), which continues along the right-hand edge of woodland, by a wire fence on the right. The path curves gradually right and, where the hedge on the left ends, bear left to continue along a parallel path, between a wire fence on the right and a hedge on the left.

After keeping through trees, the path later emerges into open country and continues along the right-hand edge of woodland to a T-junction. Turn right along the right-hand, inside edge of Menagerie Plantation, at a waymarked post turn left **B** through a clearing – a bench here acts as a useful landmark – and continue along a grassy ride, later heading downhill through trees to a

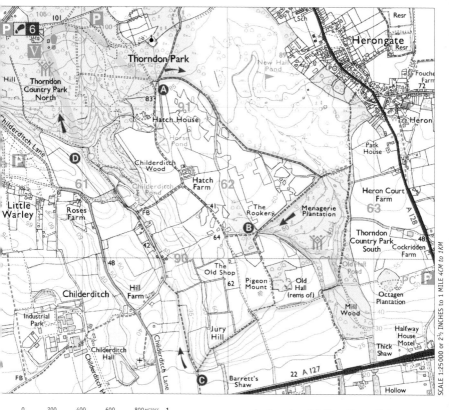

SCALE 1:25000 or 2½ INCHES to 1 MILE 4CM to 1KM

0	200	400	600	800 METRES 1

KILOMETRES
MILES

0	200	400	600 YARDS ½

T-junction in front of Old Hall Pond. Turn left, at the next T-junction turn right to cross a boardwalk and turn right again alongside the pond. At the next T-junction, turn right to continue across the far end of the pond and keep ahead to go through a kissing-gate.

Walk along a track that winds along the left-hand edge of a field. To the left are fine views looking across the Thames towards the North Downs and to the right is the site of Old Thorndon Hall – there is an information board at the far end of the field. After going through a gate, turn left along the left-hand field edge, follow the field edge to the right, go through a kissing-gate and continue along the left-hand edge of the next field. In the corner, turn left over a stile, immediately turn right, head downhill across a field to a waymarked post and follow the path to the left to continue down to a stile and public footpath sign **C**.

Climb the stile, turn right along an enclosed path and, on entering a field, bear slightly left and walk across it, continuing along its left-hand edge to climb another stile. Keep ahead to a track, turn left to cross a bridge over a stream and immediately turn right over a stile. Head diagonally across a field, climb a stile and turn right along a narrow lane. Where the lane ends, keep ahead along a tree-lined track, passing to the left of Childerditch Pond, to emerge into a meadow. Continue along the bottom right-hand edge of this sloping meadow and, in the corner, cross a plank footbridge to reach a crossroads **D**.

Keep ahead uphill into woodland again, turn left at a T-junction and follow the track around a right-hand bend. The track leads back to the start. ●

High Woods and Colchester

Start	High Woods Country Park, signposted from Colchester
Distance	4½ miles (7.2km)
Approximate time	2 hours
Parking	High Woods Country Park
Refreshments	Pubs and cafés at Colchester
Ordnance Survey maps	Landranger 168 (Colchester, Halstead & Maldon), Explorer 184 (Colchester, Harwich & Clacton-on-Sea)

On both the outward and return legs, there is a small amount of walking by trading estates and along suburban roads on the edge of Colchester but this is more than compensated for by the fine woodlands and open views at High Woods Country Park and the lovely surroundings of Castle Park in the centre of Colchester. There is also a short, pleasant stroll beside the River Colne. Be sure to allow plenty of time to explore the many historic sites and attractive old streets of Colchester, the oldest recorded town in Britain.

High Woods Country Park, around 330 acres (134 ha) of mainly woodland and grassland, is situated on the slopes of the Colne valley to the north of Colchester. In the Middle Ages it was part of the Royal Forest of Kingswood and was given to the people of Colchester by Henry VIII in 1535. It became a country park in 1987.

Start by facing the visitor centre and turn left to a junction of paths by a notice-board detailing the various waymarked walks in the country park. Take the right-hand path through the trees – signposted Circular Walk – and at a fork, continue along the right-hand path to a T-junction. Turn left along a track and, at the next T-junction on the edge of the woodland, turn right on to a hedge-lined track.

At a crossroads keep ahead along the left-hand edge of a field, go through a gate, bear right and head diagonally downhill across a field, passing between two fenced coppices. Ahead are views over Colchester. Join an enclosed path at the bottom, which bends right, by a pool on the right, to emerge on to a lane. Turn left, continue along the path ahead to pass under a railway bridge, and the path bends right – later becoming a track – to keep parallel with the railway line.

Turn left **Ⓐ** to pass beside a metal barrier, walk along an enclosed path and pass beside another barrier on to the busy main road. Cross carefully, take the enclosed path ahead, turn left at a road and at a T-junction turn right and keep ahead to enter Lower Castle Park. At a fork, take the right-hand tarmac track – this is also a cycle track – turn left at a junction and cross the bridge over the River Colne. Continue along a road by the right-hand edge of the park, which bends first left and then

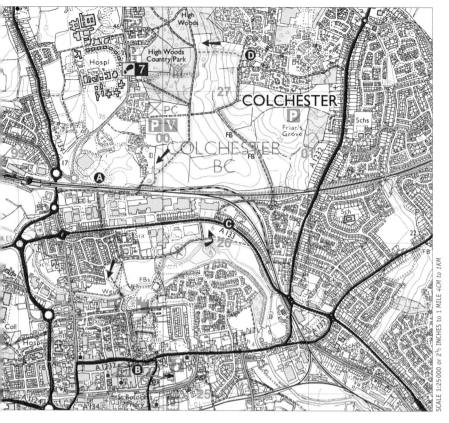

SCALE 1:25000 or 2½ INCHES to 1 MILE 4CM to 1KM

right to head gently uphill. This is
Maidenburgh Street, part of Colchester's
Dutch Quarter, so called because Dutch
refugees settled in this part of the town
in the 16th and 17th centuries. Keep
ahead, passing the 13th-century
St Helen's Church, to High Street, turn
left and bear left along Museum Street
into Upper Castle Park in front of the
keep of Colchester Castle **B**.

With its well-preserved stretches of
Roman walls, Norman castle, ruins of
St Botolph's Priory, Dutch Quarter and
narrow streets lined by attractive old
buildings, Colchester is one of the most
interesting and historic towns in the
country and merits a lengthy exploration. It was an important tribal capital –
Camulodunum – long before the
Romans arrived and made it one of
the principal cities of Roman Britain.
Over 1,000 years later, William the
Conqueror constructed the impressive

castle, the largest Norman keep in the
country, on the site of a Roman temple,
using recycled bricks and stones from
the ruined Roman city. The castle now
houses an excellent museum which
includes many Roman remains.

Keep to the left of the castle and take
the downhill path through this beautiful
park, descending steps and passing
through a gap in the Roman walls. Pass
to the right of a pool to reach the River
Colne again and turn right along a most
attractive, tree-lined riverside path. Go
through a gate to a junction, turn left to
cross a footbridge over the river and
take the right-hand path at a fork. Turn
right at a T-junction – the tarmac path
soon becomes a rough one – and follow
it around a left-hand bend to the main
road again.

Cross over, turn right in front of a retail park and at a public footpath sign to Ipswich Road turn left **C** along a tarmac path – also a cycle way. The path passes under two railway bridges, then continues parallel to the railway embankment and eventually emerges on to the end of a road. Keep ahead, turn left at a T-junction and almost immediately turn left again on to a concrete track between houses to re-enter High Woods Country Park. Pass under a railway tunnel and walk along a clear and well-defined path which curves left and right and then continues along the right-hand edge of sloping meadows to a T-junction.

Turn right and head uphill along a hedge- and tree-lined path that curves gradually left to reach a kissing-gate by a country park notice-board. Turn half-left **D** on to a worn path which heads downhill across grass and crosses a causeway near the end of the lake. Keep ahead towards woodland, turn left along a track which keeps along the left-hand, inside edge of the trees and take the first path on the right, sign-posted to Visitor Centre. The path winds back to the start. ●

Colchester Castle

Finchingfield and Great Bardfield

Start	Finchingfield
Distance	5 miles (8km)
Approximate time	2½ hours
Parking	Around The Green at Finchingfield
Refreshments	Pubs and cafés at Finchingfield, pubs at Great Bardfield
Ordnance Survey maps	Landranger 167 (Chelmsford, Harlow & Bishop's Stortford), Explorer 195 (Braintree & Saffron Walden)

There are plenty of wide and extensive views, two beautiful villages and two fine medieval churches on this walk. From the picture postcard village of Finchingfield, the route heads across fields and by the little River Pant to the almost equally attractive village of Great Bardfield. The return leg is mostly alongside Finchingfield Brook. Expect to encounter some muddy and overgrown paths in places.

Finchingfield has often been described as the prettiest village in Essex and it is easy to see why. A spacious green, lined by attractive old cottages, overlooks a duck pond and beyond the road climbs gently to the 13th- to 14th-century church. This picturesque scene is further enhanced by the 18th-century cupola on the Norman tower of the church. Pubs and cafés cater for the many visitors.

The walk starts at the junction of roads by the war memorial on The Green. Facing the pond and church, turn right along the road and, at the end of the green where the road curves slightly left, turn right, at a public footpath sign, on to an uphill tarmac drive. Where the drive turns left, keep ahead along an enclosed path which continues along the left-hand edge of a field. The path later widens into a track that

continues first between fields, then along a right-hand field edge, and bends first left and then right to reach a fork. At this point turn left off the track through a hedge gap and walk across a field corner, making for a plank footbridge on the far side. Cross it, pass through a hedge gap, turn right and walk along the right-hand edge of a field. In the corner, turn right through another hedge gap and turn left to rejoin the track.

The track heads gently downhill along the right-hand edge of the next field, goes through a gap into the next field and bears right across it down to a narrow lane Ⓐ. Turn left, keep ahead at a junction (in the Great Bardfield direction) and, where the lane curves left, turn right over a stile. Walk along the left-hand field edge, turn left over a stile and continue along a narrow path,

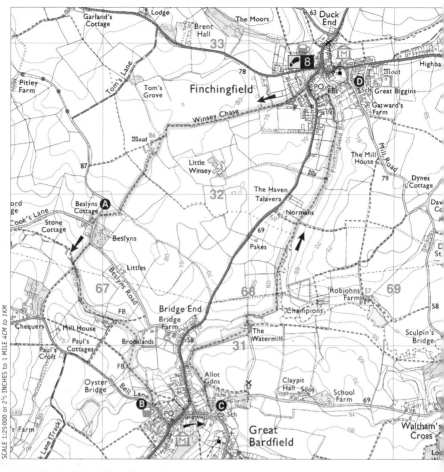

SCALE 1:25000 or 2½ INCHES to 1 MILE 4CM to 1KM

```
0      200     400     600    800 METRES  1
                                           KILOMETRES
                                           MILES
0      200     400     600 YARDS    ½
```

between a wire fence on the left and the tiny River Pant on the right, to reach a river-gauging station. Climb a stile, continue across a field, following the curve of the river to the left, and climb another stile.

Keep ahead, turn right to cross a footbridge over the river and turn left along the left-hand field edge. Follow the field edge as it curves right and look out for where you bear slightly left to climb a stile. Continue along the right-hand edge of a field, later veering left diagonally across it to climb a stile. Walk across the next field, climb a stile and head gently uphill to a pair of stiles. Climb the one in front, turn right,

head across a field and climb a stile on to a road **B**.

Turn left into Great Bardfield and at a T-junction turn left along the main street. Great Bardfield rivals Finchingfield in its attractiveness and there are some fine half-timbered cottages and handsome brick Georgian houses lining the main street.

At a fork in front of the war memorial, take the right-hand road and, at the next fork by a triangular green, take the right-hand road if you want to see the 14th-century church, otherwise the route continues along the left-hand road.

Before reaching the end of the green, turn left **C** at a public footpath sign, along a tree-lined path that emerges into a field. Keep along its winding left-hand edge, following the meanders of a stream, to climb a stile and bear right to keep by the right-hand edge of the next field. Go through a hedge gap, veer slightly left across a field, go through a fence gap and keep ahead towards a farm. After entering the farmyard, turn left to pass to the right of the house (a former mill), cross a bridge and keep ahead over another footbridge.

Turn right along the right-hand field edge, follow it to the left and, at a track, turn right and then almost immediately left to climb a stile. Walk across a narrow field, climb a stile in a fence, follow the path into the next field and keep along its right-hand edge. Finchingfield Brook is to the right, and you follow its meanders back to the village. Climb a stile, cross a plank footbridge, turn right along the right-hand edge of the next field and follow the edge to the left.

Continue along the right-hand edge of a series of fields, going through hedge gaps and small belts of woodland, and the tower of Finchingfield church comes into view. Eventually the path goes through a wood, becomes enclosed and reaches a T-junction. Turn right on to a tarmac path, cross the brook and at a tarmac track, turn right up to a road **D**. Turn left to a T-junction, turn left again, passing the church, and head downhill through the village. Cross a footbridge over the stream to return to the start.

Finchingfield

Mersea Island

Start	Cudmore Grove Country Park, signposted from B1025 immediately after crossing to Mersea Island
Distance	5½ miles (8.9km)
Approximate time	2½ hours
Parking	Cudmore Grove Country Park
Refreshments	Café at East Mersea
Ordnance Survey maps	Landranger 168 (Colchester, Halstead & Maldon), Explorer 184 (Colchester, Harwich & Clacton-on-Sea)

Mersea Island lies just off the Essex coast amidst the estuaries of the Blackwater and Colne. The first and last parts of the route are along the coast at the eastern tip of the island; the middle stretch is across meadowland, passing the old church at East Mersea. This is a walk of wide and extensive views, looking across the flat expanses of the island and the surrounding waters to the mainland.

A mixture of meadows, marshland and low cliffs make up Cudmore Grove Country Park. Between the two World Wars the area was a golf course, it later became a World War II defence site, then farmland and in 1974 was bought by Essex County Council as a place of public enjoyment and recreation.

At a sign 'Beach', head across grass to join a track and, passing to the left of a wartime pill-box, follow the track to the shore and turn left on to the sea wall **Ⓐ**. Ahead are views of Brightlingsea on the other side of the Colne estuary. The path swings left and, after just over 100 yds (91m), bear left to descend the embankment, cross a channel and walk along an enclosed path, passing to the left of a house. Keep ahead along a track to a lane, continue to where the lane bends left **Ⓑ** and keep ahead along a track to a stile. Climb it, walk along a narrow path parallel to the track and climb three stiles to enter a meadow.

Continue along the left-hand edge of the meadow and, at the corner of the wire fence on the left, keep straight ahead to a stile and fence corner. Do not climb the stile but turn right across the meadow, making for the corner of trees, where you turn left over a stile to continue along an attractive, tree-lined track. Where this track bends left, keep ahead along the left-hand edge of a meadow. At a waymarked post, keep straight ahead to the next one and then continue alongside a hedge on the right to the corner of the meadow.

Keep ahead through a hedge gap and walk along the right-hand edge of a succession of fields, passing through a series of hedge gaps.

Later follow the field edge as it curves first left and then right and finally walk along a short section of enclosed track to climb a stile on to a narrow lane. Turn left to a T-junction **Ⓒ**, turn left along the road into the hamlet of East

Mersea Island

Mersea and turn right down Church Lane to the medieval church, thought to stand on the site of a Viking camp.

Continue past the church along a tarmac drive through a holiday park, pass beside a gate and keep ahead along a hedge-lined track, which bears left to reach a section of new sea wall **D**. Turn left along it, passing in front of a beach café and chalets and, after the wall

ends, continue by the shore across a mixture of grass, sand and stones. Later continue along the beach below low cliffs – the clifftop path is not a right of way and is also dangerous because of the crumbly nature of the cliffs – to regain the sea wall near the start of the walk **A**. Immediately turn left to return to the car park.　●

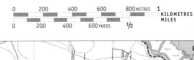

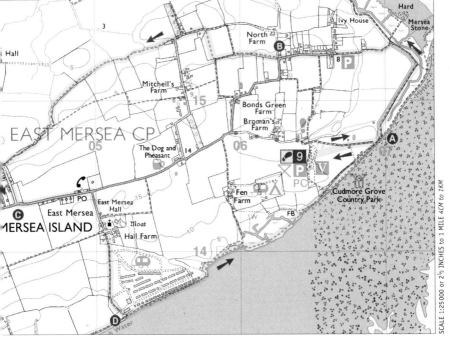

Weald Country Park

Start	Weald Country Park, Visitor Centre car park, follow signs to South Weald
Distance	5 miles (8km)
Approximate time	2½ hours
Parking	Weald Country Park
Refreshments	Light refreshments at Visitor Centre, pub at South Weald
Ordnance Survey maps	Landranger 167 (Chelmsford, Harlow & Bishop's Stortford), Explorer 175 (Southend-on-Sea & Basildon)

Lakes, woodland and grassland combine to create an attractive and satisfying walk in the Weald Country Park just to the north-west of Brentwood. There are fine views over the parkland, and in spring the woods are carpeted with bluebells. The route extends slightly northwards beyond the park to Bentley Common and also includes South Weald village.

In the Middle Ages, Weald Country Park was part of a hunting-ground, used by both medieval monarchs and the abbots of Waltham. It comprises a mixture of woodland and grassland and has two lakes, plus several ponds.

Start at the visitor centre and in the far corner of the car park – by a Country Park notice-board – take the tree-lined track which heads downhill to the lake. Cross a causeway between two lakes, turn right over a bridge and walk along a pleasant wooded path beside the lake. At the end of the lake, keep ahead across grass into woodland and turn left along a track **Ⓐ**.

Head steadily uphill, keeping close to the left-hand, inside edge of the trees, later continuing first through a belt of woodland and then along a hedge-lined track to a stile. Climb it, keep ahead to a road, cross over, walk along the tarmac drive opposite and then continue through a kissing-gate.

Continue along the left-hand edge of a field and, at a hedge corner, keep straight ahead across the next two fields, climbing stiles, and bear slightly left across the third field to another stile. Climb that, turn right along the right-hand field edge, climb a stile, continue along the left-hand edge of the next field and climb a stile on to a track **Ⓑ**.

St Paul's Church at Bentley Common is to the left but the route continues to the right along the tree-lined track called Pilgrim's Lane. It may well be muddy. In the Middle Ages this was a route taken by pilgrims on their way to Canterbury. On emerging on to a lane, turn right **Ⓒ** to a road, cross over and keep ahead along the tarmac drive to the Civic Amenity and Recycling Centre. Just before the gates to the centre, bear right beside a barrier and

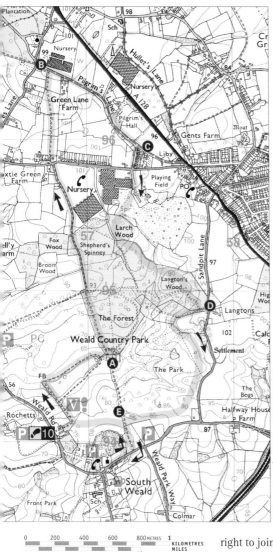

stile on to a track **D**. Turn right and look out for where a Horseride waymark directs you to turn left and head down to a gate.

Go through, turn left and keep along another undulating path, which winds along the left-hand edge of grassland, in and out of trees, curving right just before reaching a barrier. The path continues along the edge of the park, bending right again to keep parallel to a road and later bearing right away from the road. At a fork – just before reaching two fairly close waymarked posts – take the right-hand path across grass (do not turn left to a road), which later keeps to the right of a cricket field to reach a gate. Go through, continue along an enclosed path, which turns left to another gate, go through that, turn right to join a track and keep ahead to a Country Park notice-board **E**.

For a brief detour into South Weald, turn left, walk across the grass to pass through a fence and turn right on to a path above the road to the church and pub. South Weald church was mainly rebuilt in the 19th century but retains its fine medieval tower. Return to the Country Park notice-board and keep ahead through the fence gap beside it. Bear left, in the direction of the visitor centre, to head across grass to the start, enjoying the grand views to the right across the park, with the lake below and woodland on the horizon. ●

SCALE 1:25000 or 2½ INCHES to 1 MILE 4CM to 1KM

bear right again along a path which curves left.

Follow this winding path into woodland to a T-junction, turn left and after a few yards turn left again through a blue-waymarked gate and take the path ahead. The rest of the route follows blue 'Horseride' waymarks through the Country Park. Continue through mixed woodland, turning right along the left-hand edge of the trees to a T-junction. Turn left and keep along a winding and undulating path to eventually climb a

Pleshey and Great Waltham

Start	Pleshey
Distance	5½ miles (8.9km)
Approximate time	2½ hours
Parking	Roadside parking at Pleshey
Refreshments	Pubs at Pleshey, pub at Great Waltham
Ordnance Survey maps	Landranger 167 (Chelmsford, Harlow & Bishop's Stortford), Explorer 183 (Chelmsford & The Rodings)

The outward route is along the south side of the valley of Walthambury Brook between Pleshey and Great Waltham. The return follows the well-waymarked Essex Way along the north side, keeping by the brook for much of the way. There are fine views across the valley, and on the final part of the route you walk beside the medieval earthworks that enclose the village of Pleshey.

Pleshey is a most attractive and interesting village with a sloping main street lined by old cottages – some of them thatched – the moat and earth-works of a Norman castle, and a hand-some, mainly Victorian church, built on the site of its medieval predecessor. In addition the whole village is enclosed by a defensive earthwork, probably constructed around the same time as the castle, which is followed on the last leg of the route.

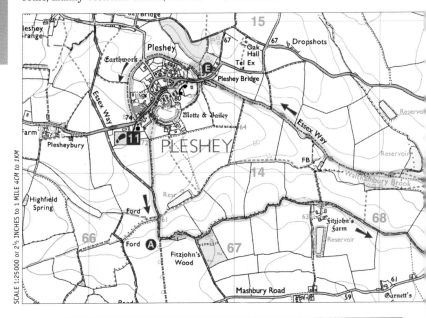

The walk starts by the church at the top end of the village. With your back to it, turn right down The Street and, at a public footpath sign, turn right along Pump Lane. This soon becomes a track and over to the left is the moat and earthworks of Pleshey Castle, built in the 12th century. At a public footpath sign, bear right off the track, head diagonally across a sports field and in the corner, pass beside a hedge gap on to a concrete track. Continue along the track – initially along the right-hand edge of a field, later enclosed – ignore the first public footpath sign on the left but at the second one, turn left **A** along a pleasant, hedge- and tree-lined bridle-way. At a fork by the corner of wood-land, take the left-hand track along the left-hand edge of the wood, continue along it, sometimes along field edges but mostly enclosed, and it curves right to a T-junction in front of a house.

Turn left and continue along a hedge-lined track, which bends right to a lane **B**. Turn left and follow the lane (Barrack Lane) to the right into Great Waltham to reach a T-junction by the pub and opposite the church. The church is basically Norman, though much restored, and nearby is a hand-some Elizabethan timber-framed house. At the T-junction turn left and, soon after crossing a bridge over Waltham-bury Brook, turn left over a stile **C** and walk along the right-hand edge of a field. From here the well-waymarked Essex Way is followed back to Pleshey.

Cross a lane **D** and take the path ahead, which bends left and then curves right to keep below the embankment of a pool, bending right again and turning left at a T-junction. Continue along a track and, in the field corner, turn left and then curve right, this time to keep below a reservoir embankment. At the corner of the embankment, turn left across the field to a public footpath sign and turn right to continue along the left-hand field edge. For most of the remainder of the walk you keep beside Walthambury Brook.

Keep along the left-hand edge of fields as far as a waymarked post, where you cross the brook and continue along the right-hand edge of fields, eventually emerging on to a road **E**. From here there are two equally attractive routes back to the start. The first is to turn left and walk up through the village, passing Pleshey Mount Viewing Area, where there is a fine view of the castle mound and an information board. The second is to follow the line of the village earthworks.

For the second alternative, cross the road and take the path opposite, which curves gradually left, following the ditch and tree-lined embankment of the earthworks. Cross a lane and continue by the embankment, still curving gradu-ally left all the while. After crossing a plank footbridge, keep ahead to emerge on to the road opposite the church. ●

Hatfield Forest

Start	Hatfield Forest, car park on lane signposted to Bush End and Hatfield Forest from A120 at Takeley
Distance	5½ miles (8.9km)
Approximate time	2½ hours
Parking	Hatfield Forest
Refreshments	Café by lake in Hatfield Forest
Ordnance Survey maps	Landranger 167 (Chelmsford, Harlow & Bishop's Stortford), Explorers 183 (Chelmsford & The Rodings) and 195 (Braintree & Saffron Walden)

The first part of this flat and easy walk is across fields to join the Flitch Way, a disused railway track. You then follow the tree-lined way along the edge of Hatfield Forest before entering it. The remainder of the route is across the grassy plains, by the lake and through the woodlands of the forest, one of the finest and least altered survivals of the medieval Forest of Essex. Do not let the sound and sight at times of planes landing and taking off from nearby Stansted Airport put you off what is a most attractive and satisfying walk.

Along with Epping and Hainault, Hatfield Forest is one of the surviving remnants of the Forest of Essex, a vast royal hunting-ground which in the Middle Ages extended over much of the county. As a result of careful and traditional methods of management over the centuries, it is little changed and probably resembles a medieval forested area more closely than any-where else in the country. In 1729 the forest was acquired by the Houblon family, who were responsible for the lake and Shell House. It is now managed by the National Trust and because of its unique landscape value it has been designated a National Nature Reserve.

Begin by leaving the car park and turning right along the lane, passing a tiny church. Turn left along the lane signposted to Bush End **Ⓐ** and, where it bears right, turn left over a stile and take the path ahead across a field. Climb a stile on the far side, walk along the left-hand edge of a field to a T-junction and turn left on to a track, which bends right to continue along the right-hand edge of a field. Where the track turns left, keep ahead along a path to continue by field edges and, in the corner of the last field, turn right and then immediately left through a hedge gap on to a straight, tree-lined path **Ⓑ**.

This is the Flitch Way, a footpath and cycle way created from the former Braintree to Bishop's Stortford Railway. After crossing a bridge over a lane, the path continues along the right-hand edge of Hatfield Forest. At a Forest Way post, turn left **Ⓒ** over a stile, in the Epping Forest direction – here joining

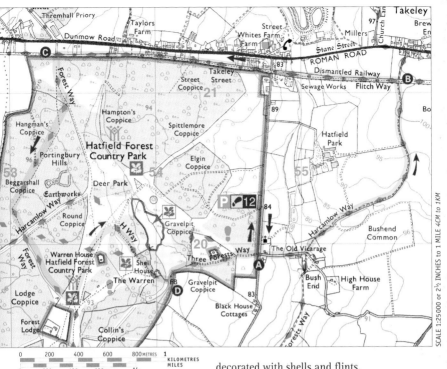

the Forest Way and entering the forest –
and keep ahead along a faint grassy
path across an open area. At the second
Forest Way post, follow the direction of
the yellow waymark to the right, keep
ahead at a crossroads (by the corner of
a wire fence on the left) and the path
bears left to another crossroads.

Keep ahead to eventually emerge into
a large open area and bear
left across it to meet a
stony track. Turn left
along this curving track to
a T-junction and turn
right along a tarmac drive
to a car park and National
Trust information board
by a junction of tracks
and paths. Turn left
through a gate and take
the path that passes in
front of the café and Shell
House. The latter, an
18th-century picnic room,
is so called because it is

decorated with shells and flints.

Bear left **D** to continue across the
end of the lake and, immediately on
entering woodland, turn right through
trees to a stile. Climb it, keep ahead past
some impressive ancient trees and bear
left to a T-junction. Turn right, climb a
stile to emerge from the woodland and
keep ahead to climb another stile on to
a lane **A**. Turn left to return to the
starting point. ●

In Hatfield Forest

St Osyth Creek

Start	St Osyth
Distance	6 miles (9.7km)
Approximate time	3 hours
Parking	St Osyth, by Priory Gatehouse
Refreshments	Pubs and cafés at St Osyth, pub at Point Clear
Ordnance Survey maps	Landranger 168 (Colchester, Halstead & Maldon), Explorer 184 (Colchester, Harwich & Clacton-on-Sea)

There are wide and extensive views across meadows, creeks and marshes as you walk along the path beside St Osyth and later Brightlingsea creeks to the martello tower near Point Clear. This is followed by nearly 1¹⁄₂ miles (2.4km) of quiet road walking. A final stretch across fields and by the end of Mill Dam Lake leads back to the start. An alternative route, retracing your steps along the creekside path, is provided for those who prefer to avoid the road walking.

The small village of St Osyth is dominated by its priory, founded in the early 12th century as a house of Augustinian canons. After its dissolution in 1539, a large house was built on the site, incorporating many of the monastic structures, and this was subsequently extended both in the 18th and 19th centuries. The 15th-century gatehouse – where the walk begins – is considered one of the finest in the country and is the main survival of the medieval monastery. Almost opposite is the mainly Tudor parish church.

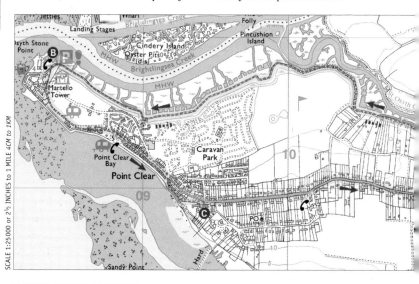

St Osyth Creek

Facing the priory gatehouse, turn left along the road, which bears left to cross a bridge over the end of Mill Dam Lake. On the other side, turn right **Ⓐ** at a public footpath sign, along a path that keeps along the edge of the marshes beside St Osyth Creek and follow this winding path – mainly along the top of an embankment and through several kissing-gates – for almost $2^{1}/_{2}$ miles (4km). Towards the end you pass beside a large caravan park on the left and to the right the views are dominated by the docks at Brightlingsea.

Eventually the path curves left around St Osyth Stone Point and continues – now concreted – in front of chalets and bungalows. When you see a martello tower on the left, turn left **Ⓑ** off the coast path and walk along a track, passing to the left of both the Ferry Inn and the martello tower. The latter is now an aviation and 1940s museum.

At this point, those who wish to avoid about $1^{1}/_{2}$ miles (2.4km) of road walking can retrace their steps to the bridge over the end of Mill Dam Lake **Ⓐ**. *Turn right along the road and rejoin the main route by turning left along a narrow lane where the road bends right* **Ⓓ**.

For the main walk, continue along the track through part of the caravan park and between houses to a road at Point Clear. Keep ahead to a junction, bear right along a tarmac drive (Sea View Terrace) and continue along a gently ascending path above a beach. The path bears gradually left to rejoin the road **Ⓒ** and you keep along it to where it bends to the left **Ⓓ**.

Bear right here along a narrow lane and across the fields to the left, the houses, church and priory gatehouse at St Osyth can be seen slightly elevated above the surrounding countryside. Where the lane bends right, keep ahead along a track across fields and, just before reaching the corner of a field, turn left on to a track, which heads towards St Osyth. Descend to cross a bridge over the end of Mill Dam Lake, ascend to a farm and continue between farm buildings to emerge on to the road opposite the start. ●

Great Dunmow and Little Easton

Start	Great Dunmow
Distance	5½ miles (8.9km)
Approximate time	2½ hours
Parking	Great Dunmow
Refreshments	Pubs and cafés at Great Dunmow, pubs at Church End
Ordnance Survey maps	Landranger 167 (Chelmsford, Harlow & Bishop's Stortford), Explorer 195 (Braintree & Saffron Walden)

The Flitch Way, a former railway track, is used for the first part of the walk. You then head across fields to the delightful church at Little Easton and continue along tracks and field paths to Great Dunmow's church, over ½ mile (800m) north of the town centre at Church End. The final leg is across meadows beside the River Chelmer.

The walk begins in the Market Place at Great Dunmow by the attractive, half-timbered Elizabethan Old Town Hall. The town is particularly renowned for the ancient custom of the Dunmow Flitch, which consists of awarding a flitch of bacon to a newly married couple who can satisfy the judges that they have managed to live together for a year and a day following the marriage without an argument. The Flitch Trials, revived in the Victorian era, are held every leap year.

Start by turning left along the main street, in the Chelmsford direction, turn right by the war memorial into New Street and at a Flitch Way sign, turn right along a tarmac path **Ⓐ**. Where the path emerges on to the end of a road, bear right to continue along an enclosed, partially tree-lined path and pass beside a barrier on to a road. Turn left and, where the road turns left, keep ahead to pass beside another barrier and walk along an enclosed tarmac path, passing houses and the end of a road to a stile.

Climb the stile, descend steps to carefully cross the busy A120, ascend steps opposite, go through a kissing-gate and turn right **Ⓑ** along a tree-lined track. This is the Flitch Way, which follows the line of the former Braintree to Bishop's Stortford Railway. At first the route keeps along the top of an embankment – at one stage there is a boardwalk over a boggy area – later you continue through a cutting, pass under a bridge and keep ahead to a gate. After going through it, turn right along a track, recross the A120 and turn left. At a public bridleway sign, turn right **Ⓒ** along the left-hand edge of a field, by the side of High Wood, go through a hedge gap in the field corner and keep ahead across the next field. Continue along the right-hand edge of trees and finally walk along a short

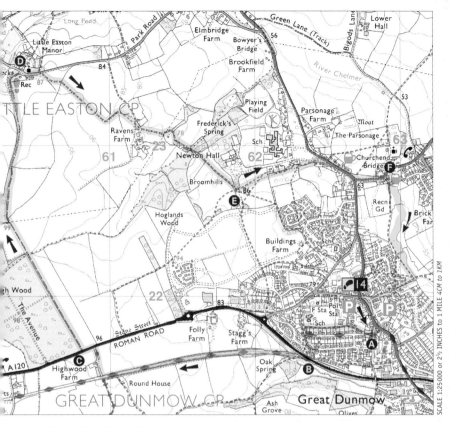

SCALE 1:25000 or 2½ INCHES to 1 MILE 4CM to 1KM

0   200   400   600   800 METRES   1
                              KILOMETRES
                              MILES
0   200   400   600 YARDS   ½

stretch of enclosed path, curving right to emerge on to a lane by the delightful little church at Little Easton **D**.

The church dates from the Norman period but was partially rebuilt in the 13th and 15th centuries. Inside there are some splendid tombs and monuments, a 12th-century wall-painting and some 14th-century frescoes. More recent memorials are two stained glass windows that commemorate the 386th United States Bomber Group, which was stationed at Little Easton in the Second World War.

Turn right and, at a public footpath sign just beyond the church, bear right to follow a track across a field, keeping to the left of a group of trees to reach a waymarked post. Continue in the same direction to a T-junction and turn left

on to a track that bears right to a house. Cross a tarmac track to the right of the house, walk along the concrete track opposite and, in front of a gate, bear left along a track, by a fence on the right. Bear right to continue along the right-hand edge of a field, go through a kissing-gate and head uphill.

At the top, keep along the right-hand field edge, and the track bears left **E** beside trees on the left to a waymarked post. Head across the field to climb a stile, keep ahead by garden fences and hedges on the left and continue across to a stile by another waymarked post. After climbing it, walk along a track and turn right beside a spacious green to reach a road near the Cricketers pub. Keep ahead and where the main road bends right, turn left, in the Great Bardfield and Finchingfield direction.

The road bends left in front of the Angel and Harp pub to St Mary's, the mainly 14th-century parish church of Great Dunmow, but the route continues along a track **F** to the right of the pub. The track bears right in front of a house to a kissing-gate. Go through, bear left across a meadow beside the River Chelmer, pass through a hedge gap and continue across the next meadow to join the river. Keep beside it to a tarmac path by a footbridge and turn right.

At a fork immediately ahead, take the left-hand path, which heads gently uphill to pass beside a barrier. Keep ahead to a road, continue gently uphill to a T-junction and bear right to return to the Market Place.

The River Chelmer near Great Dunmow

Thaxted

Start	Thaxted
Distance	6½ miles (10.5km)
Approximate time	3 hours
Parking	Thaxted
Refreshments	Pubs and cafés at Thaxted
Ordnance Survey maps	Landranger 167 (Chelmsford, Harlow & Bishop's Stortford), Explorer 195 (Braintree & Saffron Walden)

This walk takes you through the pleasant, gently rolling countryside of the Chelmer valley to the north, west and south of Thaxted. For part of the way the tower and spire of Thaxted church and the nearby windmill serve as landmarks. Be prepared for some of the narrow paths to be muddy after rain and overgrown during the summer. It is worth while allowing time for an exploration of Thaxted, a particularly attractive small town.

One of the largest and finest parish churches in the country rises above Thaxted and the surrounding country-side. The reason why a small town should boast such a magnificent church is that in the later Middle Ages Thaxted thrived as a centre for both the cutlery and woollen industries. The church was rebuilt on its present lofty and spacious lines in the 14th century and has a 181ft- (55m) high tower and spire.

The superb, timber-framed, 15th-century Guildhall below the church and other fine buildings in the town centre also reflect Thaxted's medieval prosperity. A plaque on the wall of a house in Town Street records that it was the home of the composer Gustav Holst, and it is thought that he wrote part of the Planets Suite while there.

The walk starts in front of the Guild-hall. Walk up the main street to the right of it, passing the church, to the Bull Ring and just after the main road

bends right, turn left **Ⓐ** along a lane signed 'Watling Street, Cul de Sac'. The lane bends right, at a fork take the left-hand lane, heading downhill, and the lane narrows to a track and crosses the infant River Chelmer. Where it turns right to a house, keep ahead along a track, which bends left and continues along the right-hand edge of a field.

The route then continues along a narrow, enclosed path and, on emerging from this, turn right, walk across a field and pass through a hedge gap on the far side. Continue along the left-hand edge of a young plantation, then along an enclosed path, go through another hedge gap and keep ahead to a T-junction. Turn left along a track, passing to the left of a barn, and the track becomes enclosed. At the end of the enclosed section, keep ahead along a concrete track, bear left on joining another one and follow it to a road **Ⓑ**.

Turn left and, at a public footpath

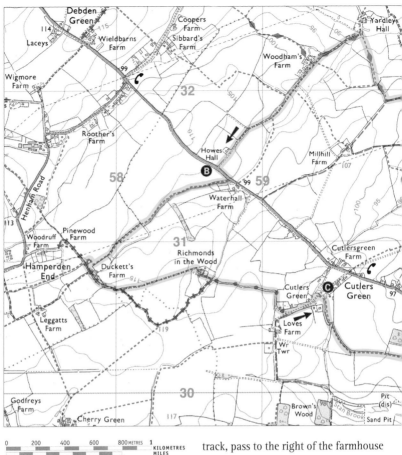

sign, turn right and walk along the left-hand edge of fields. Keep ahead through a hedge gap, cross a plank footbridge, climb a stile and continue along the right-hand edge of the next field. In the corner, turn right over a stile, turn left along the left-hand field edge, turn right in the corner to continue along the left-hand edge of the next field and just beyond the corner of a high wire fence, turn left to a track. Turn left along it, passing a farm. Where the track turns right into a field, keep ahead along an enclosed, tree-lined path.

On emerging into a field, keep along its left-hand edge, and the path then continues between fields towards a farm. At a waymarked post to the left of the farm buildings, turn right on to a track, pass to the right of the farmhouse and continue along a drive, which bends first right and then curves left to a T-junction. Turn left along a narrow lane and, at a public footpath sign, turn right **C** on to a path, which becomes enclosed and continues through a belt of woodland to emerge into a field.

Turn left along another short enclosed stretch and then bear right to walk along a left-hand field edge. Go through a hedge gap, turn left to pass through another gap and follow a wide grassy track along the left-hand edge of a field. After going through another hedge gap, head gently downhill along the left-hand edge of the next field and over to the left is a fine view of Thaxted church and windmill. In the bottom corner, keep ahead along an enclosed track, do not join a tarmac drive but

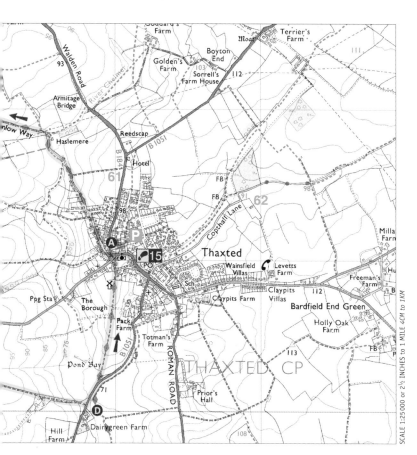

continue along the enclosed track that keeps parallel to the drive, eventually emerging on to it and continuing down to a road **D**.

Turn left and where the road curves slightly right – just before the gate to a house – turn left through a hedge gap. Walk along a path that passes to the left of the house and heads gently uphill along the right-hand field edge directly towards the windmill and church. The windmill was built in 1804 by John Webb, a local farmer, on the site of an earlier one.

Pass to the right of the windmill to join an enclosed tarmac path and go through a kissing-gate. Keep ahead in front of a row of cottages, go through another kissing-gate and continue between cottages and in front of the church to a road. Turn right downhill to the start.

Thaxted church

Castle Hedingham and the River Colne

Castle Hedingham and the River Colne

Start	Castle Hedingham
Distance	6 miles (9.7km)
Approximate time	3 hours
Parking	Roadside parking at Castle Hedingham
Refreshments	Pubs and café at Castle Hedingham, pub at Sible Hedingham
Ordnance Survey maps	Landranger 155 (Bury St Edmunds, Sudbury & Stowmarket), Explorer 195 (Braintree & Saffron Walden)

This figure-of-eight walk in the Colne valley starts with a circuit of Castle Park, the wooded parkland surrounding the remains of Hedingham Castle. The rest of the route is across fields and through woodland, including a short but attractive stretch beside the placid River Colne. There are fine views over the valley but some parts of the walk are likely to be muddy and/or overgrown at times.

There are some delightful old houses and cottages in Castle Hedingham, which lies at the foot of the wooded hill occupied by the great castle. The church is an unusually fine and interesting example of an almost complete Norman village church, with a superb late 12th-century nave and chancel. At the east end is a rare Norman wheel window.

Hedingham Castle is one of the grandest and best preserved Norman keeps in the country. It was built in 1140 for the powerful De Veres, earls of Oxford, and still stands to its full height of 110ft (33m). Its interior probably gives visitors a better idea of a Norman castle than anywhere else, and the carved stonework and great cross arches in the great hall are normally only seen in the finest cathedrals.

The walk begins in the main street by the Bell Inn and post office. With your back to the inn, turn left, follow the road around a left-hand bend and turn right down Church Lane. Turn right, passing the church, and keep ahead along Crown Street to a T-junction **Ⓐ** Take the path ahead – not the parallel drive to the right of it – which passes to the right of Pye Cottage, and this attractive, hedge- and tree-lined path heads gently uphill to a stile. After climbing it, keep ahead across a field to the end of a hedge, continue uphill alongside the hedge and climb a stile at the top.

Turn right along a winding lane and, at a public footpath sign opposite Rosemary Farm, turn right on to a path which continues between fields. Keep ahead along a narrow enclosed path that heads downhill through woodland

SCALE 1:25000 or 2½ INCHES to 1 MILE 4CM to 1KM

0	200	400	600	800 METRES	1
					KILOMETRES
					MILES
0	200	400	600 YARDS	½	

bordering Castle Park and pass beside a barrier on to a road. Turn left and look out for steps and a public footpath sign on the right **B**. Climb the steps and walk first along an enclosed path and then along a right-hand field edge to a waymarked post. Turn left, continue across the field towards a farm and head down into a dip, passing to the right of a solitary tree. Do not climb the

stile at the bottom of the field but turn right along its left-hand field edge and follow it – there are several twists and turns – to a road.

Cross over, walk along a tarmac track and, soon after passing to the right of Maiden Ley Farm, you join the well-waymarked Hedingham Mills Walk **C**. The track bears left and, where it ends, keep ahead along a rough track to a fork. Take the right-hand enclosed path along the left-hand edge of woodland, which turns right to a stile. Climb it and

The River Colne near Castle Hedingham

over a stile **E**. Walk across a field to a hedge corner, keep by the hedge on the left to join the river and continue beside it as far as a field corner. Turn left away from the river, walk along the right-hand edge of fields and, on joining a track, turn right through a hedge gap **F** – here leaving the Hedingham Mills Walk – and follow a track across a field.

cross a plank footbridge. Turn left to continue across rough meadowland, bear right through trees to climb a stile and keep ahead to a lane **D**. Turn right, cross a bridge over a disused railway track and, at a public footpath sign, turn left along a track, passing between cottages.

At a waymarked post, turn left to walk along the right-hand edge of a field, follow the edge as it curves first right and then left, pass beside a barrier and continue along a fence-lined path. Keep along the narrow, enclosed path to enter woodland and continue through it to a T-junction. Turn right along a track, at a fork keep ahead along the right-hand track and, at the next fork, take the narrower left-hand path. The path heads gently uphill, re-enters trees and continues up through this most attractive woodland. It then turns right to keep along the left-hand edge of the wood and emerges, via a barrier, on to a lane.

Turn right down this narrow lane and cross a bridge over the disused railway again. Turn right by Hull's Mill, a 19th-century rebuilding of an earlier mill, and just after crossing a footbridge over the River Colne by a ford, turn right

Continue along a path by the right-hand edge of the next two fields and, in the corner of the second field, pass through a belt of trees and keep along the right-hand edge of the next field. The path bears right through another belt of trees and curves left to reach a lane in front of Alderford Mill **G**. Turn left along the lane if you want the pub in Sible Hedingham but the route continues to the right to cross a bridge over the Colne. Here you rejoin the Hedingham Mills Walk and follow it back to the start.

Beyond the bridge you temporarily rejoin the outward route and retrace your steps to point **C** just before Maiden Ley Farm. Turn left here off the tarmac track and walk along a path that keeps along the right-hand edge of a pool. The path then winds through trees and bushes, crosses a plank footbridge and keeps along the right-hand edge of woodland. As you later continue along the left-hand edge of a field, the top of the keep of Hedingham Castle can be seen across the field to the right.

The path eventually reaches a road just to the right of a brick bridge. Turn right and follow it back into Castle Hedingham. ●

Benfleet Downs and Hadleigh Marsh

Start	Hadleigh Castle Country Park, Chapel Lane car park
Distance	6½ miles (10.5km). Shorter version 4½ miles (7.2km)
Approximate time	3 hours (2 hours for shorter walk)
Parking	Hadleigh Castle Country Park
Refreshments	None
Ordnance Survey maps	Landranger 178 (Thames Estuary, Rochester & Southend-on-Sea), Explorer 175 (Southend-on-Sea & Basildon)

From both the hilltop vantage points on this walk – near Chapel Lane car park and at Hadleigh Castle – there are splendid views across Canvey Island and the Thames estuary to the North Downs on the horizon. The views also extend along the river from Southend to Canary Wharf. After descending from the car park, the route keeps along the base of the wooded Benfleet Downs and continues across marshes alongside Benfleet Creek before climbing back to the start. The shorter version omits the loop that takes in the ruins of Hadleigh Castle.

Start by heading across to the corner of the car park, where there is a 'Way-marked Trails' notice-board and a map of the country park, go through a kissing-gate and keep ahead to a T-junction. Turn left along a path through woodland, heading downhill to go through a kissing-gate, and continue downhill across a field, making for the right-hand edge. Keep along the edge, in the 'Hadleigh Castle via Marsh' direction, to the bottom right-hand corner, go through a hedge gap, continue by a hedge on the right and bear slightly right to go through another wide hedge gap.

Continue to a kissing-gate, go through, cross a track and go through another kissing-gate opposite. Keep ahead – across grass and between hedges – go through a kissing-gate and, at a footpath post, turn right Ⓐ in the South Benfleet direction. The route continues across marshland and, after going through a kissing-gate, along the edge of the woodlands of Benfleet Downs to another kissing-gate. Go through that, keep ahead parallel to the railway line, and eventually the path turns left to cross the railway Ⓑ.

Turn left along a tarmac drive, between the railway on the left and Benfleet Creek on the right, climb a stile beside white gates, keep ahead along the drive – Benfleet Moorings are on the right – and turn left to go through a kissing-gate. The route now continues along the top of a broad embankment above Hadleigh Marsh. To the right is Benfleet Creek and Canvey Island, to the left the wooded slopes of Benfleet Downs, and ahead Hadleigh Castle and the buildings on the edge of Southend-on-Sea.

Keep along this embankment for 1 mile (1.6km) to where it bears left and turn left here **C** on to a grassy path which descends from the embankment and crosses a causeway over a channel to a stile. Climb it, continue across the marsh, skirting a wire fence, recross the railway line and keep ahead to a T-junction. Turn right along the edge of the marsh, climb a stile, keep ahead to climb another and continue along the bottom edge of a sloping field to a public footpath sign to Chapel Lane **D**.

*Turn left here for the shorter walk and follow directions from where point **D** next appears in the text.*

For the full walk to Hadleigh Castle, keep ahead, between a wire fence and a hedge, climb a stile and continue along the left-hand edge of Hadleigh Marsh. After climbing another stile, keep ahead along a right-hand field edge, below the castle, and in the corner follow the field edge to the left to a stile. Do not climb it but turn left **E** and follow a worn path uphill across grass, continuing along a broad ridge towards the castle. Go through a kissing-gate, keep alongside a metal fence on the left bordering the castle and climb a stile on to a track **F**. Although there is considerably less of Hadleigh Castle now than when Constable painted it, the remaining walls and towers still make an imposing sight above the marshes of the Thames estuary. The castle was built by Hubert de Burgh in the 13th century and partially rebuilt by Edward III in the 14th century.

After climbing the stile on to a track, turn sharp left to climb another one and head downhill along a track. In front of a metal gate at the bottom, turn right to a stile, here rejoining the previous

route, and retrace your steps to the public footpath sign to Chapel Lane **D**.

Turn right, here picking up the shorter walk, and head gently uphill alongside a wire fence on the right. Climb a stile, continue uphill by the right-hand field edge, climb another stile and keep ahead by the right-hand edge of the next field to a footpath post. Bear right to the next footpath post, keep ahead along the left-hand field edge, below a reservoir embankment, climb a stile in the field corner and bear left along a track.

After climbing a stile, turn right along a track, passing to the right of farm buildings, and continue along a lane. Take the first turning on the left to return to the start. ●

Hadleigh Castle

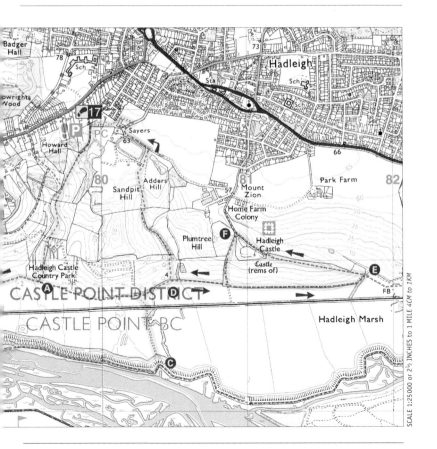

Mill Green and Blackmore

Start	Millgreen Common, parking area on the common almost opposite the Cricketers pub
Distance	6½ miles (10.5km)
Approximate time	3½ hours
Parking	Millgreen Common
Refreshments	Pub at Mill Green, pubs at Blackmore
Ordnance Survey maps	Landranger 167 (Chelmsford, Harlow & Bishop's Stortford), Explorer 183 (Chelmsford & The Rodings)

Much of the walk is through attractive woodlands which, like Millgreen Common, are surviving remnants of Writtle Forest. In between there are extensive views over open country, and the route passes through the attractive village of Blackmore with its fine medieval church. Most of the route is along broad and clear tracks but there are some narrow paths in places.

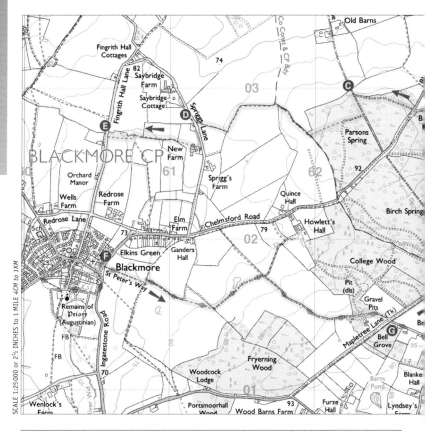

Millgreen Common is a small remnant of the medieval royal hunting-ground of Writtle Forest, and its landscape of woodland and open grassland can have changed little since the Middle Ages.

Start by returning to the road almost opposite the Cricketers pub, turn left and, at a public bridleway sign, turn left **A** along a track through woodland.

Follow this undulating track to where it emerges from the trees and keep ahead across a field to a road. Turn left, follow the road around a right-hand bend and, at a public bridleway sign, turn left **B** along a broad track (Metsons Lane), passing through a timber yard. Continue along the right-hand, inside edge of Barrow Wood to a road, cross over to a public footpath sign and walk along a path through more woodland to reach a concrete track **C**. Turn left and, after about 100 yds (91m), turn right over a plank footbridge and continue along a winding path through dense woodland. At a footpath post, turn left to cross a plank footbridge and climb a stile to emerge from the trees.

Turn right along the right-hand edge of rough grassland and, at the far, tapering corner of the field, keep ahead through a hedge gap, climb two stiles in quick succession and continue along the right-hand edge of the next field. Follow the field edge to the left, turn right over a stile, turn along the left-hand edge of the next field and, in the corner, turn right and continue along the left-hand field edge to a lane **D**. Turn left along the tree-lined lane and, at a public footpath sign, turn right on to a track, passing between farm buildings to a gate. Go through, keep ahead to go through another gate and continue along the left-hand edge of a field.

Go through a hedge gap, cross a plank footbridge, keep along the left-hand edge of the next field but, after about 20 yds (18m), turn left through another hedge gap and climb a stile. Continue by the right-hand field edge, at a fence corner keep ahead across the field to regain the field edge and climb a stile on to a lane **E**. Turn left and at a crossroads keep ahead into Blackmore to reach another crossroads in the village centre.

The route continues to the left but it is worthwhile keeping ahead along picturesque Church Street to visit Blackmore's mainly Norman church. Its most striking feature is the tall, pagoda-shaped, 15th-century timber tower and spire. The church was originally built to serve an Augustinian priory and became a parish church after the priory,

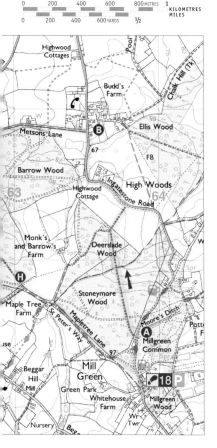

of which there are virtually no remains, was dissolved in 1527. Henry VIII was a frequent visitor to Blackmore as he had a mistress here.

At the crossroads turn left by The Green to a T-junction, turn left and, at a public footpath sign, turn right  through a hedge gap and walk across a field, making for a waymarked post on the far side. Go through a hedge gap, turn left along the left-hand edge of the next field, follow the edge to the right and, at a hedge corner, keep ahead across the field to a footpath post. Go through another hedge gap, bear slightly left across the next field, skirting the right-hand edge of a pond,

and continue across to a track on the far side. Turn right to continue first along the left-hand edge of fields, then through woodland (passing to the left of pools) and bear right to reach a crossroads Ⓖ.

Turn left, at a public bridleway sign, on to a path that keeps along the right-hand, inside edge of College Wood to a T-junction and turn right Ⓗ in the Mapletree Lane direction, along a broad, tree-lined track. At a fork, take the right-hand track, which continues along the right-hand, inside edge of more fine woodland and, where it bears left, keep ahead beside a barrier and take the grassy path across Millgreen Common to return to the start. ●

In Blackmore

Coggeshall and Feering

Start	Coggeshall
Distance	7½ miles (12.1km)
Approximate time	4 hours
Parking	Coggeshall
Refreshments	Pubs and cafés at Coggeshall, pub at point **C**, pub at Feering, pub at point **H**
Ordnance Survey maps	Landranger 168 (Colchester, Halstead & Maldon), Explorer 195 (Braintree & Saffron Walden)

This is a walk of wide and extensive views in the gentle landscape of the Blackwater valley to the east and south of Coggeshall. It is mostly across fields and there is a particularly attractive stretch beside the river near the end. Historic interest is provided by the fine medieval churches at Coggeshall and Feering, plus Paycocke's House and the monastic barn and chapel near Coggeshall.

In the Middle Ages, Coggeshall was second only to Colchester in Essex as a prosperous centre of the cloth trade and it has a number of attractive, timber-framed buildings that reflect this. Largest and most impressive of these is Paycocke's, built around 1500 by Thomas Paycocke, a wealthy merchant clothier. The clock tower in the town centre was built to commemorate Queen Victoria's Golden Jubilee in 1887.

Start at the junction of roads in the town centre and walk along Church Street, passing to the right of the large 15th-century 'wool church'. Turn right at a T-junction and, at a public footpath sign opposite St Anne's Close, turn left **A** through a gate to join the Essex Way. Walk along a narrow, tree-lined path, keep ahead across a field, go through a hedge gap and continue along the left-hand edge of the next field. Go through another hedge gap and ascend steps to the main road. Cross

over, descend steps opposite, climb a stile and walk along a left-hand field edge.

Keep ahead at a crossroads to continue along the left-hand edge of the next field but look out for where an Essex Way sign directs you to turn left down steps. Go through a hedge gap, cross a plank footbridge and turn right along a right-hand field edge. On reaching a lane, turn right **B** – here leaving the Essex Way – to a T-junction, turn right along a main road and turn left along a lane **C** beside the Porter House Inn. Where the lane curves slightly left, bear right to a public bridleway sign and walk along a tree-shaded enclosed path. A stretch along the right-hand edge of a field is followed by another enclosed path before emerging on to a lane **D**. Turn left to a T-junction and turn right, in the Feering and Kelvedon direction, along a narrow, winding lane.

After about ¾ mile (1.2km) – just after passing South Cottage – turn right

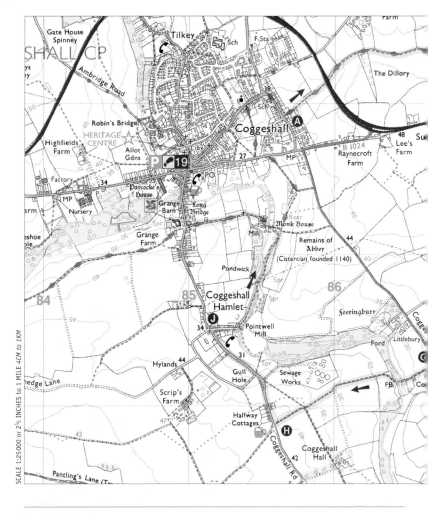

The River Blackwater

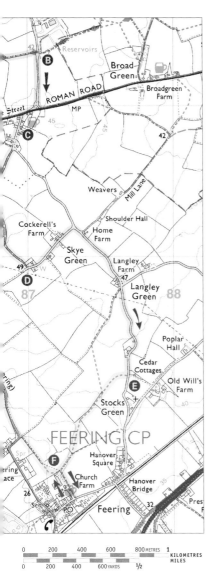

Retrace your steps to point **F** and continue across the field, then along its left-hand edge, and in the corner keep ahead to a road. Turn right and, at a public footpath sign, turn left along a track **G**. Where the track ends at a cottage, continue through trees along the right-hand one of two paths ahead and cross a footbridge over the River Blackwater. Keep ahead to enter a field but, after a few yards along its right-hand edge, turn right over a plank footbridge and turn left along an enclosed path. The route now continues along the left-hand edge of a succession of fields – there is a track at one point – finally going through a gate on to a road opposite the George and Dragon pub **H**.

Turn right into Coggeshall Hamlet and at a No Through Road sign, turn right **J** along Pointwell Lane. Where the lane ends, keep ahead along a track, passing in front of the former Pointwell Mill, and cross a bridge over the river. Bear right to cross another bridge and go through a gate. Now follows a delightful part of the route as you walk across meadows beside the tree-lined bank of the Blackwater. Cross a footbridge over the channel that has been on your right, keep ahead and, at the end of the meadow, climb a stile and continue to a T-junction.

Turn left along a track, recross the river, bear right through a farmyard and continue along the track, passing to the left of an isolated 13th-century chapel. This was the gatehouse chapel of the now vanished Coggeshall Abbey. The track reaches a road in front of Coggeshall Grange Barn, another monastic survival. Now owned by the National Trust, it dates from the 12th century and is reputedly the oldest surviving timber-framed barn in Europe.

At the road turn right, cross the Blackwater once more and keep ahead into Coggeshall. ●

E at a public footpath sign, on to a grassy path that heads across fields, later continuing by a right-hand field edge. After going through a hedge gap, bear left and walk diagonally across a field towards Feering church, pass through a wide gap and continue across to the corner of the next field **F**. For a short detour into Feering, turn left along the right-hand field edge and turn right along a road into the pleasant village, which has a pub and 15th- to 16th-century church.

Newport and Debden

Start	Newport, Station car park
Distance	6½ miles (10.5km)
Approximate time	3½ hours
Parking	Newport Station
Refreshments	Pub at Newport, pubs at Debden
Ordnance Survey maps	Landrangers 154 (Cambridge & Newmarket, Saffron Walden) and 167 (Chelmsford, Harlow & Bishop's Stortford), Explorer 195 (Braintree & Saffron Walden)

By Essex standards this is a relatively hilly walk, rising to 345ft (105m) on the first part of the route between Newport and Debden. The return leg takes you across part of Debden Park and then on through the valley of Debden Water. Both Newport and Debden are attractive places with fine medieval churches.

The long main street in Newport is lined by handsome buildings dating from the late medieval period to the 19th century. Foremost amongst these is the brick and timber-framed, 15th-century Monk's Barn. The 13th- to 15th-century church has an imposing tower built in 1858.

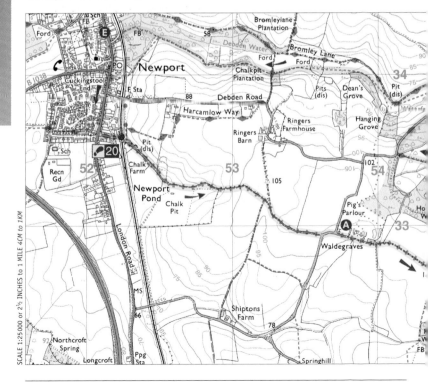

Start by crossing the station foot-bridge, keep ahead to a tarmac track and turn right. At a public bridleway sign by the entrance to a huge chalk quarry, turn left along a pleasant, hedge- and tree-lined path, which heads uphill to emerge into a field. Keep along the left-hand edge of the field, following it as it curves right, to a lane, turn left and, where the lane turns left, keep ahead **A** along the track to Waldegraves Farm.

Continue along the track, passing along the right-hand edge of Cabbage Wood, and at a fork take the right-hand track to continue by the edge of the wood. Look out for where a waymarked post directs you to turn first left and then right and then head gently downhill along the right-hand edge of a field to reach a lane by a picturesque, black-and-white thatched cottage.

Turn left and, at a public footpath sign, turn left again **B** to walk along the right-hand edge of a field. Just before reaching the corner, turn right over a footbridge and turn left to keep along the left-hand edge of the next field, by woodland on the left. The path continues first along the right-hand, inside edge and later the left-hand, inside edge of the woodland, then becomes enclosed and bears left through a hedge gap. Turn right along the right-hand field edge, follow the edge to the left and continue up to a lane **C**. Turn right here for a short detour into the pretty village of Debden which has a pond, thatched cottages and a pub.

Retrace your steps along the lane and continue to the entrance to Debden churchyard. The church, which stands in a beautiful and isolated setting, dates mainly from the 13th century. Bear right along a path by the right-hand edge of the churchyard, turning first left and then right to continue along the right-hand edge of trees to a T-junction by a pool on the left. Turn left to cross a bridge between pools, keep ahead along a track and, at a footpath sign, turn right to follow a path across Debden Park. To the right is a view of the lake.

At the far end of the field, keep ahead over a stile and walk along the left-hand edge of the next field to a metal kissing-gate. Go through and keep ahead to go through another one on to a road. Turn right downhill, cross Debden Water and continue gently uphill to a public footpath sign **D**. Turn left here and, at a fork immediately ahead, take the left-hand track. Climb a stile, walk along the left-hand edge of a field, bear right through a gate and keep along the right-hand edge of the next field to climb another stile. The path now curves along the right-hand field edge to a fork. Take the left-hand path, pass through a gap into the next field and curve left by the edge of woodland to continue across the middle of the field to a stile.

Climb it, keep ahead across a field, making for the corner of trees, and continue by the trees to a crossing of paths. Keep ahead beside conifers to the corner of the field and continue gently uphill along a broad, grassy ride between trees. As you keep along the winding right-hand edge of the next field, by trees on the right, the top of the tower of Newport church comes into view. Climb a stile in the field corner, keep ahead through woodland, turn left to cross a footbridge over the infant River Cam and turn right to continue under a railway bridge.

Keep ahead along a tarmac track to the main street in Newport and turn left **E**. At the far end of the village, turn left again to return to the station.●

A lane near Debden

Stour valley: Constable Country

Start	Manningtree Station
Distance	7½ miles (12.1km)
Approximate time	4 hours
Parking	Manningtree Station
Refreshments	Pubs and cafés at Dedham, café at Bridge Cottage by Flatford Mill
Ordnance Survey maps	Landranger 168 (Colchester, Halstead & Maldon), Explorer 196 (Sudbury, Hadleigh & Dedham Vale)

This classic walk is in the Stour valley on the Essex-Suffolk border, immortalised in the paintings of John Constable. An undulating route along the well-waymarked Essex Way, mainly via tracks and field paths, brings you to Dedham. The walk then continues by the winding River Stour through Dedham Vale, the heart of Constable Country, passing the landmarks of Flatford Mill and Willy Lott's Cottage before returning to the start. Pick a fine day and take time to enjoy this outstanding walk to the full.

With your back to the station building, take the path signposted to Flatford and Dedham down to a T-junction and turn right along a tree-lined track. At a footpath post, turn left **A** in the Lawford church direction, along an enclosed path, which heads steadily uphill, bends right and then left to reach the church.

Go through a gate into the churchyard, pass to the right of the church and the path bears left to exit the churchyard by another gate. Head across to public footpath and Essex Way signs, bear right to a field corner and continue into trees to a stile. Climb it, keep ahead to climb another, walk across the corner of a field and climb a stile on to a track. Turn left along the straight, tarmac track, go through a kissing-gate and turn right along a road.

Follow the road around a left-hand bend and after ¼ mile (400m), bear left **B** at a public bridleway sign, along an enclosed track to a gate. Go through, continue along the enclosed track and turn left through a gate. Walk along a track, passing to the left of a cottage, and bear left on joining another track. Follow the track around a right-hand bend, keep ahead at a crossroads and the track bears right down to a farm. At an Essex Way sign, bear right off the track, walk across grass to enter woodland and continue gently downhill to cross a plank footbridge.

Climb a stile, keep ahead across a field to climb another, carefully cross a railway line, climb two stiles in quick succession and keep straight ahead across a field to another one. Climb it – and another immediately in front – keep ahead between fences to climb another stile and continue along an enclosed path to a road. Cross over, climb the stile opposite, bear slightly left across a field to the corner and climb a stile on to a lane.

Turn right and the lane curves left and continues through trees. Where it bends right, keep ahead **G** over a stile, head gently uphill along the left-hand edge of a field, climb a stile and keep ahead over the brow to climb two more stiles. Walk along a right-hand field edge, climb a stile, continue across the middle of the next field, later keeping along its right-hand edge. In the corner, go through a gate and keep ahead along a track to a road. Turn right, at a public footpath sign turn left **D** over a stile and walk across a field, heading down to a footpath post on the far side.

Continue down into woodland, climb a stile and keep along the bottom, inside edge of the wood, turning left to pass in front of a house.

Turn right along a drive to a tarmac track, turn right, passing cottages, and at a public footpath sign, turn left along a tarmac track between more cottages. Go through a gate, pass in front of a farmhouse, turn right through another gate and keep ahead to a stile. After climbing it, walk along the left-hand edge of a field, climb a stile, cross a plank footbridge, bear right and head diagonally across the next field. Climb a stile in the corner, head across two fields, going through two kissing-gates and continue along a right-hand field edge.

In the field corner, keep ahead to climb a stile into a sports field and turn

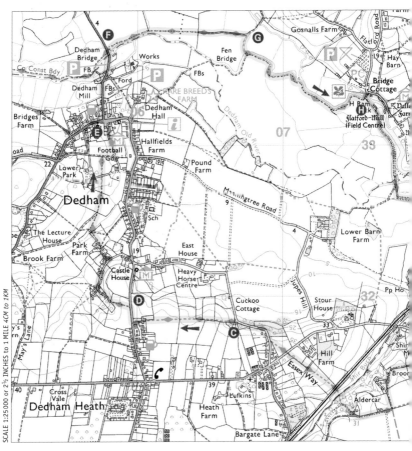

right along its right-hand edge, passing behind the cricket pavilion, to a tarmac path. Turn left along the tree-lined path, passing beside a barrier to emerge on to a road in the centre of Dedham **E**.

From the 14th to the 17th centuries this small town was a flourishing centre of the cloth trade and has a wealth of attractive buildings. These range from late medieval timber-framed houses to dignified Georgian residences. The large 'wool church' was built in 1492 and has an imposing west tower. Constable attended the local grammar school.

Keep ahead along Mill Lane, passing Dedham Mill and cross bridges over first a channel, then the main River Stour and finally another channel, here briefly entering Suffolk. At a public footpath sign to East Bergholt and Flatford, turn right **F** through a kissing-gate and walk across riverside meadows beside the Stour, later bearing away from the river to a kissing-gate on the far side of the meadow. Keep ahead along a tree-lined path to a T-junction, turn sharp right **G** on to another tree-

lined path and go through a kissing-gate to cross Fen Bridge over the Stour, here re-entering Essex.

Turn left down steps and go through another kissing-gate. Now comes a delightful part of the walk as you continue across meadows by the winding river through a typical Constable landscape. After climbing a stile in front of a wooden footbridge **H** the route continues to the right, still beside the river, but it is worthwhile crossing the bridge to Bridge Cottage and turning right along a lane for a short distance to see Flatford Mill and Willy Lott's Cottage.

All these properties, now owned by the National Trust, feature in Constable's paintings. Bridge Cottage houses a Constable exhibition and has a pleasant tearoom. Both Flatford Mill and Willy Lott's Cottage are leased to the Field Studies Council and are not open to the public. Constable's father owned Flatford Mill and others in the Stour valley.

After turning right in front of the footbridge, at a public footpath sign to Manningtree, walk along a tree-lined path, passing Flatford Lock. A little further on is a fine view across the river of Flatford Mill. Continue along the path and later you pass to the right of a concrete barrier. Cross a bridge over a channel by a lock and keep ahead beside the barrier to a kissing-gate. Turn left through it and walk along the top of a low embankment above pastures and marshland. Go through two more kissing-gates and, just after the second one, turn right at a public footpath sign to Manningtree Station.

Go through another kissing-gate and along an enclosed path that turns first left and then right, widens into a track and passes under a railway bridge. Just beyond the bridge, turn left along a tree-lined track parallel to the embankment, which leads back to the start. ●

Audley Park and Wendens Ambo

Start	Saffron Walden
Distance	7½ miles (12.1km). Shorter version 3 miles (4.8km)
Approximate time	3½ hours (1½ hours for shorter walk)
Parking	Saffron Walden
Refreshments	Pubs and cafés at Saffron Walden, pubs at Wendens Ambo, café at Audley End House
Ordnance Survey maps	Landranger 154 (Cambridge & Newmarket, Saffron Walden), Explorer 195 (Braintree & Saffron Walden)

Saffron Walden is situated at the gates of Audley Park, and you quickly gain access to paths that take you across the splendid parkland and over the River Cam, with grand views of Audley End House. The route then heads across to the picturesque village of Wendens Ambo, on the other side of the valley, before returning for a final stroll across the park. The shorter walk is simply a circuit of Audley Park and omits Wendens Ambo. Leave plenty of time to explore Saffron Walden, a most appealing town.

Saffron Walden is an outstandingly attractive town with a wealth of fine old buildings, a reflection of its importance and prosperity in the Middle Ages as a centre of the cloth industry. It was also the main centre for the production of the saffron crocus – hence the word saffron in the name of the town – grown locally as a medicine and as a dye for the cloth trade. Dominating the town is the magnificent church, a tall and spacious building of cathedral-like proportions, mostly built between 1450 and 1525. The spire was added in 1832. Nearby are the remains of the Norman castle keep and a medieval turf maze. Be sure to take a look at the fascinating Old Sun Inn, a group of 14th-century houses with some outstanding pargetting (moulded plasterwork) from the 17th century.

Start in the Market Place by the late 18th-century Town Hall (now the tourist information centre) and, facing the library, walk along the street to the left of it. Turn left at a T-junction, take the first turning on the right (Abbey Lane), pass some almshouses and keep ahead to go through a metal gate, here entering the Audley End estate **Ⓐ**.

At a fork immediately ahead, take the right-hand path and at the next fork take the right-hand (narrower) path again and follow it across Audley Park. Cross a footbridge, pass through a line of trees and continue between fences to a kissing-gate. Go through, and the path continues along the right-hand edge of the park, gradually curving left. Over to the left are fine views of Audley End House. Look out for where a yellow waymark directs you to keep

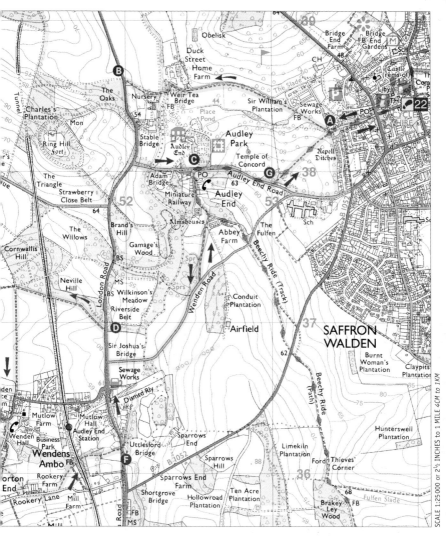

SCALE 1:25000 or 2½ INCHES to 1 MILE 4CM to 1KM

0	200	400	600	800 METRES	1	
						KILOMETRES
						MILES
0	200	400	600 YARDS		½	

ahead to a metal kissing-gate, go through and walk along a tree-shaded path, by a wall on the left, to join a tarmac drive.

Keep along the drive, cross a bridge over the River Cam and continue up to a road **B**. Turn left, take the first lane on the left, cross Adam Bridge – from here there is a superb view of the house – and continue past the visitor entrance to Audley End House to a tarmac track on the right, signposted to the College of St Mark **C**.

Audley End House, an outstanding example of Jacobean architecture, was built in the early 17th century by Lord Howard of Walden, 1st Earl of Suffolk, on the site of a medieval abbey. It was a huge palace, one of the largest in the country – almost twice its present size – and was even a royal palace for a while, bought by Charles II in 1669 but returned to the Howard family in 1701. In the 18th century it was partially demolished and then remodelled, with some of the rooms designed by Robert Adam. The formal gardens are superb, and the park, one of the finest in the country, was landscaped by 'Capability' Brown.

Wendens Ambo

Continue along the lane if doing the short walk.

For the full walk, turn right gently downhill along the tarmac track, passing between rows of attractive old cottages, and at a fork in front of the college entrance, take the left-hand track. Where the track turns left, keep ahead across grass, by a wall on the right, to a waymarked post and follow more of these posts through a farmyard. Continue along the right-hand edge of a field, by woodland on the right, to a road and turn right. The road bears right to cross the River Cam again and heads up to a T-junction. Turn right and, at a public footpath sign at the corner of a wood, turn left **D** through a gate and walk along the right-hand edge of a field, by the woodland on the right.

In the field corner, keep ahead to cross a railway bridge, continue along the right-hand edge of the next field but, just before the field edge bears slightly left, turn left and head straight across the field. From this reasonably elevated position there are fine all-round views. Continue down a sunken, hedge-lined track to a road in the village of Wendens Ambo and keep ahead. On the left you pass a lane, lined on one side by picturesque thatched cottages, that leads to the attractive flint church. This dates from the 12th century and retains its Norman tower but was partially rebuilt and extended later in the Middle Ages.

Where the road curves right to the Bell Inn, turn left along a lane and, just after crossing a footbridge by a ford, turn left over a stile **E**. Walk along the right-hand field edge, negotiate two stiles in quick succession (plus the intervening plank footbridge) and bear left across a field to climb another stile. Keep in the same direction across the next field and on the far side cross a track to a gate. Go through, climb a stile a few yards ahead, continue along a fence-lined path, go through a gate and turn left to a lane.

Turn left along this narrow lane and, at a public footpath sign, bear left along a fence-lined path. Keep ahead through trees, turn right at a waymarked post to pass under a railway viaduct and continue, by a stream on the left, to a stile. Climb it, keep beside the stream to climb another stile, continue along a fence-lined path and climb a stile on to a road **F**. Turn left, walk past the Fighting Cocks and turn right along the road signposted to Saffron Walden and Audley End House.

At this point you rejoin the outward route and retrace your steps to the lane in front of Audley End House **G**.

Turn right – here leaving the outward route and rejoining the short walk – keep by the boundary wall of Audley Park on the left and, after just over ¼ mile (400m), turn left through a metal gate and under an arch to re-enter the estate **G**. Walk across the park in a straight line towards the buildings of Saffron Walden – the church spire can be seen ahead – and after going through a metal gate on the far side, retrace your steps through the town to the start. ●

Ingatestone and Mountnessing

Start	Ingatestone
Distance	8½ miles (13.7km)
Approximate time	4½ hours
Parking	Ingatestone
Refreshments	Pubs and cafés at Ingatestone, pubs at Mountnessing
Ordnance Survey maps	Landranger 167 (Chelmsford, Harlow & Bishop's Stortford), Explorer 175 (Southend-on-Sea & Basildon)

There are wide and unimpeded views on this highly enjoyable walk in the undulating country that lies just to the north of Brentwood and Billericay, and there is a real feel of remoteness at times. It is also full of interest and includes two halls, three churches and a windmill. The route is on good paths and is well-waymarked throughout.

Ingatestone's long High Street is lined by a mixture of buildings, including timber-framed ones dating from the 16th and 17th centuries and some fine Georgian houses. The small, pleasant town is dominated by the tall, red brick tower of its imposing medieval church, and inside are tombs of the Petre family, who lived in the nearby hall.

The walk starts in the main street in front of the church. Take the path up to it, bear right in front of it and go through a kissing-gate into a recreation ground. Keep ahead along a tarmac path but at a fence corner on the left, bear left to continue along the edge of a cricket field and turn left at another hedge corner to cross a railway bridge. Go through a gate and keep ahead across fields to a stile. Climb it, keep by the left-hand field edge and at a fork by a fence corner **Ⓐ** continue along the right-hand path, bearing right to

emerge on to a lane in front of Ingatestone Hall. The house, built in the 16th century by Sir William Petre, has an impressive long gallery and some fine Tudor panelling.

Turn left, at a public footpath sign turn right over a stile and walk along the right-hand field edge to a stile. Climb it, keep ahead across the next field and, on the far side, climb a stile, ascend steps and carefully cross the railway line. Descend steps on the other side, turn left below the embankment, turn right over a stile and walk along an enclosed path to a road. Turn left, turn right along an enclosed tarmac track, at a Brentwood Circular Walk sign, and continue along a road to a T-junction.

Turn right, immediately turn left **Ⓑ** to cross a bridge over the A12 and turn right along Trueloves Lane. Follow the lane around a left-hand bend and, at a public footpath sign, turn left **Ⓒ** on to a

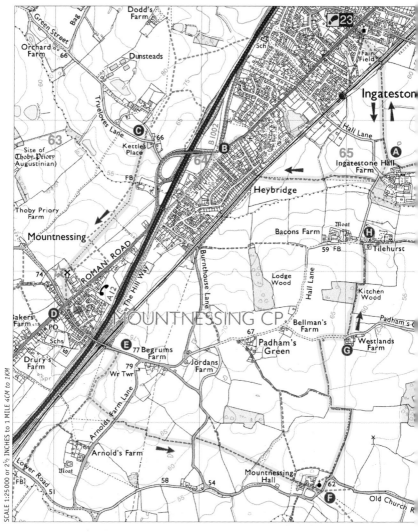

path that heads gently downhill across a field. The houses and windmill at Mountnessing can be seen on the ridge ahead. After crossing a footbridge over a brook, continue gently uphill, and the path bears right to head towards the windmill. At the far end of the field, go through a hedge gap into Coronation Playing Field and turn left to pass to the left of the early 19th-century windmill. Pass between gateposts, keep ahead to go through a fence gap and at the corner of a hedge, bear left across the playing-field to the road in Mountnessing **D**.

Continue along Church Road (sign-posted to Billericay) and shortly after recrossing both the A12 and the railway line, turn right **E** at a public footpath sign and walk across a field, passing to the right of two isolated trees. Keep ahead beside a ditch to a waymarked post, turn left to cross a footbridge over the ditch and continue across a field to a lane. Cross over and take the path almost opposite across the next field to emerge on to another lane. Turn left and, at a public footpath sign, turn right and head straight across fields towards Mountnessing church, crossing two footbridges. Continue along a track, passing farm buildings and in front of Mountnessing Hall, and continue along

```
0    200   400   600   800 METRES  1
                                    KILOMETRES
                                    MILES
0    200   400   600 YARDS   1/2
```

a tarmac drive, to the right of the church, to a road **F**. The 13th-century church served the medieval manor of Mount-nessing, based on the hall, which is why it is some distance from the present village. The hall was the home of the Mountneys, who gave their name to the area, and the present building is mainly Elizabethan with a Georgian façade.

Turn left and, where the road bends right, bear slightly left at a public bridleway sign, and walk along the right-hand edge of a field. Turn left in the field corner, at a T-junction turn right and continue along a tree-lined path. Keep ahead along a track across fields and, where the track bends right in front of a house, continue along an enclosed path to a lane. Turn right and, at a public bridleway sign, turn left **G** along a left-hand field edge and bear right to a waymarked post. Continue along the left-

hand edge of the next field, by Kitchen Wood on the left, turn right in the corner and, where the hedge on the left ends, turn right to keep along the right-hand edge of a field. Turn right **H** on to a tarmac track – soon Ingatestone Hall is seen over to the left – and where this track ends, turn left along a path by a ditch on the right.

Follow the ditch to the right, turn left in the field corner and continue along-side the River Wid. Turn right to cross a footbridge over the river and turn left along a lane up to Buttsbury church, whose wooden tower has been in sight for much of the last $1/2$ mile (800m). This small, isolated church has a 14th-century nave and 18th-century chancel. At a junction of lanes, turn left **J** alongside a hedge on the right, passing to the left of the church, and at a hedge corner, keep ahead downhill across a field to rejoin the riverbank.

Keep along it to a footbridge, turn left to cross the river and take the track ahead across fields to Ingatestone Hall. Just before reaching some barns, bear right along the right-hand field edge and bear right again on joining another path **A**. Here you rejoin the outward route and retrace your steps to the start.   ●

Mountnessing windmill

Burnham and the River Crouch

Start	Burnham-on-Crouch
Distance	8½ miles (13.7km)
Approximate time	4 hours
Parking	Burnham-on-Crouch
Refreshments	Pubs and cafés at Burnham-on-Crouch
Ordnance Survey maps	Landranger 168 (Colchester, Halstead & Maldon), Explorer 176 (Blackwater Estuary)

The first and last parts of the walk are along promenades and embankments beside the River Crouch and there are wide views, especially looking across the estuary to the desolate and uninhabited marshes of Wallasea Island on the other side. In between, the route heads inland across fields and along lanes, doing a loop around the edge of Burnham and passing its imposing medieval church, about 1 mile (1.6km) north of the present town centre.

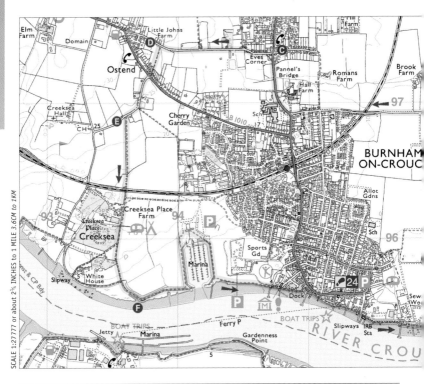

Many handsome and attractive old buildings line the river and quayside at Burnham-on-Crouch. The town developed as a port in the Middle Ages when the original settlement moved away from the church – about 1 mile (1.6km) inland – to the river.

The walk begins in the town centre by the Victorian Clock Tower. Turn down Shore Road (signposted to Ferry and Quay) to the river and turn left along the paved promenade beside it. After the promenade ends, keep ahead along the top of the sea wall, following it around several small creeks. There are fine and expansive views both inland over reclaimed marshland and across the estuary. After about 2 miles (3.2km), look out for a stile below on the left and descend from the embankment – there are some steps cut into the turf – to climb it **A**.

Walk along a track, by a drainage channel on the left, and where the track turns right, keep ahead along a path, still beside the channel. In the field corner bear left to join another track and, after passing a public footpath sign, the route continues along a straight concrete track across fields. Ignore the first public footpath sign on the right but, at the second one, turn right along the left-hand edge of a field. Turn left at a waymarked post, continue along a straight path, passing an isolated tree, and at a T-junction, turn right along the left-hand edge of a field, beside a line of trees.

Pass through a hedge gap, keep straight ahead across the next field and, on the far side, turn right along a track. Where the track turns left towards a farm, turn left on to a parallel path, which keeps along a right-hand field edge to emerge on to a narrow lane **B**. Turn left, cross a railway bridge and keep ahead to a T-junction. Turn right,

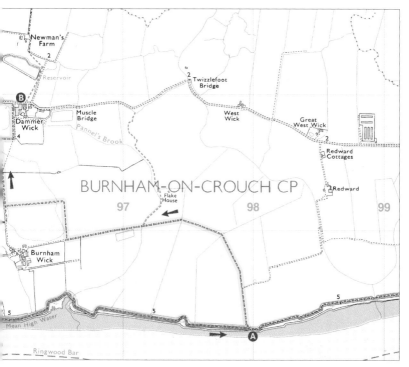

passing Burnham's large and impressive mainly 14th-century church, and at a crossroads turn left along Green Lane **C**.

After ¹/₂ mile (800m), turn left **D** over a plank footbridge, at a public footpath sign Creeksea No. 2, and walk along a path to a road. Keep ahead along Creeksea Lane, following it around a right curve, and at a public footpath sign, turn left **E** and walk along the right-hand edge of a field. Keep ahead across the next field to cross a railway line and continue along the right-hand edge of fields towards the River Crouch. On reaching the riverside embankment, bear left along it **F** and, apart from having to make a wide detour around a marina, you keep by the river back to Burnham.

After the marina, the route continues along a tarmac path and, on reaching the town, the path twists and turns between boatyards and cottages and along the quayside. Between Ye Olde White Harte Hotel and the Anchor, turn left along Shore Road to return to the starting point.

Burnham-on-Crouch

Maldon and the Blackwater estuary

Start	Maldon, Promenade Park
Distance	9 miles (14.5km)
Approximate time	4½ hours
Parking	Promenade Park at Maldon
Refreshments	Pubs and cafés at Maldon, pubs and café at Heybridge Basin
Ordnance Survey maps	Landranger 168 (Colchester, Halstead & Maldon), Explorer 183 (Chelmsford & The Rodings)

A combination of busy quaysides and boatyards, marinas and quiet river and canalside meadows, plus extensive views across the Blackwater estuary, makes for an exceptionally enjoyable and varied walk. The route also passes through the centre of Maldon, a delightful old town well worth exploring. Much of the walk is beside water: either the Blackwater estuary, River Chelmer or the Chelmer and Blackwater Navigation.

Begin by facing the estuary and heading across to the far right corner of the car park. Turn right along a tarmac track, turn left to the riverside promenade and turn left along it. Ahead is a superb view of Hythe Quay and St Mary's Church.

The quay was at its height in the 17th and 18th centuries when Maldon was a major port and it is still used today by some of the Thames sailing barges. St Mary's Church dates from the late 12th century but the original tower fell down in 1596 and was rebuilt in brick in 1636. The distinctive octagonal spire, added in 1740, was a valuable landmark for sailors navigating the Blackwater estuary.

The promenade curves right between the river and a pool and emerges on to a road. Turn left **A** beside the Jolly Sailor Inn, passing to the right of St Mary's

Church, turn right at a T-junction into Maldon town centre and walk up High Street. Most of the town's main historic buildings are in High Street, and you pass – in order – the early 18th-century Plume Library, built on the site of the medieval St Peter's Church, the 15th-century Moot Hall, and the 13th-century All Saints' Church.

At All Saints' Church, turn right **B** along Silver Street, which curves left and continues as Beeleigh Road. Where the road ends, keep ahead along a track but almost immediately bear slightly left to continue along a parallel, enclosed path, which later heads gently downhill under a green canopy to a stile. After climbing it, descend steps to cross carefully the busy bypass, ascend the steps opposite and climb another stile. Walk along an enclosed path, climb a stile and keep ahead across an enclosed grassy area to climb another stile in the left-hand corner. Continue along an enclosed path, passing to the left of Beeleigh Abbey, a private house built on the site of a 12th-century Premonstratensian monastery.

Continue along a tree-lined tarmac drive to a narrow lane **C**, turn right and, where the lane ends, keep ahead along a hedge- and tree-lined track. After this track bends right, keep ahead through a metal kissing-gate and along a wooded path to cross a footbridge over the River Chelmer by a weir. Turn right beside the river, go through a kissing-gate to reach the Chelmer and Blackwater Navigation by a lock, turn right on to a tarmac path and cross a bridge by another weir. The complex of waterways around here is known as the Beeleigh Falls.

Passing to the right of a brick bridge, continue along a tarmac track beside the Chelmer and Blackwater Navigation, opened in 1797 to provide a direct link between Chelmsford and the sea. To the right is Maldon golf course and, where the track bears right to the club house, keep ahead along a path beside the canal and turn left over the next bridge **D**. Turn right along the other bank and go under the bypass.

You now keep beside the canal to where it empties into the Blackwater estuary at Heybridge Basin, a distance of about 2 miles (3.2km). At first the route is through the outskirts of the town, passing by industrial estates, but later the surroundings become more rural. At Heybridge Basin, turn right **E** to cross the lock gates and walk along an embankment by the estuary. Follow the river around a right-hand bend and continue along the embankment, between the estuary on the left and a lake formed from a flooded gravel pit on the right. There are fine views across the water to Maldon. The

embankment eventually narrows to a path that bears right to emerge on to a track. Turn left to a road, turn left along it to a main road **F** and keep ahead to a T-junction. Turn left back into Maldon – keeping ahead all the time and following signs to Town Centre, and after crossing the bridge over the River Chelmer, turn left **G** along Fullbridge Quay, passing between boats and cranes.

Continue along Chandlers Quay and, where the road ends, keep ahead – first along an enclosed path and later a tarmac drive – to emerge into Downs Road. Keep ahead, at a crossroads continue along The Hythe, and at the Jolly Sailor Inn **A** you pick up the outward route and retrace your steps back to the starting point at Promenade Park .

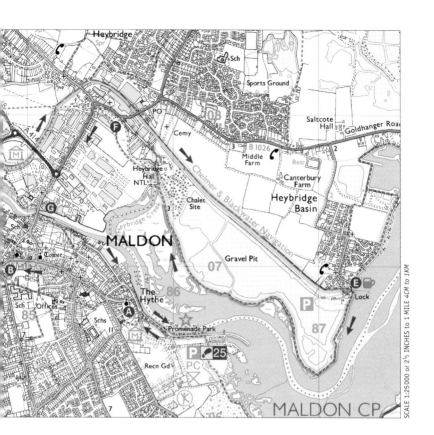

Maldon

White Notley and Cressing

Start	Cressing Station, signposted from B1018 south of Braintree
Distance	9½ miles (15.3km). Shorter version 7½ miles (12.1km)
Approximate time	5 hours (4 hours for shorter walk)
Parking	Parking area by Cressing Station, on west side of level-crossing
Refreshments	Pub at The Green, pub at White Notley, pubs at Cressing
Ordnance Survey maps	Landranger 167 (Chelmsford, Harlow & Bishop's Stortford), Explorers 195 (Braintree & Saffron Walden) and 183 (Chelmsford & The Rodings)

This is a lengthy but relatively undemanding walk, mainly along well-signed tracks, field paths and quiet lanes, in the pleasant countryside of the Brain valley to the south of Braintree. It passes through two attractive villages, both with traditional Essex churches, and includes a detour to the interesting Cressing Temple. The shorter version omits this detour.

Turn right out of the parking area to go over the level-crossing and walk along the lane to a T-junction. Turn right, in the Witham direction, and at a public footpath sign just before a farm **A**, turn sharp right over a stile and walk along the right-hand edge of a field. Go through a hedge gap, cross a track and keep by the left-hand edge of the next field, bearing right before the field corner to a stile.

Climb the stile, cross a railway line, climb the stile opposite and continue gently downhill across a golf course. Cross a ditch, turn right, then turn left to cross the second footbridge over the little River Brain and keep ahead to pick up a grassy path – marked by a line of blue stakes – which continues gently uphill across the golf course to a stile. After climbing it, keep ahead across a field and climb another stile on to a

road at The Green **B**. Turn right and almost immediately turn left, at a public footpath sign, on to a path that heads across a field, bearing slightly right to continue by a ditch on the right.

In the corner, turn left to walk along the right-hand field edge and look out for where the path turns right to cross a ditch. Turn left to keep along the left-hand edge of the next field, follow the field edge to the right and continue along the winding edge to the next corner. Turn left here along a track to a lane, turn right and take the first track on the left. The track winds between fields and, about 50 yds (46m) after passing a barn on the right, turn left on to a concrete track, which later continues as a pleasant grassy track along the left-hand edge of fields. The track eventually becomes tree-lined and bends left to a fork. Take the right-hand track to emerge on to a road and turn right **C** into White Notley, an attractive village with a fine medieval church. At a T-junction, turn left along a lane, in the Silver End and Cressing direction, and cross a bridge over the River Brain **D**.

At this point, those wishing to do the shorter walk should keep ahead along the lane.

For the full walk, immediately turn right – here joining the Essex Way – head across grass and continue along a track to a metal kissing-gate. Go through, walk along a straight, hedge-lined tarmac track, climb a stile and continue along the left-hand edge of a field. Climb another stile, walk along the left-hand edge of the next field and keep ahead, passing a footbridge over the River Brain, to a waymarked post. Turn left here and head gently uphill along the right-hand edge of a field, climb a stile and recross the railway line. Climb the stile opposite, keep ahead to climb another and walk across the next field to emerge on to a road opposite Cressing Temple. Climb the stile opposite, turn right along a fence-lined path and turn left to the entrance **E**.

Cressing Temple originally belonged to the Knights Templars but after the order was suppressed by the Pope in 1308, it passed to the Knights Hospitallers.

On the banks of the little River Brain near White Notley

SCALE 1:25000 or 2½ INCHES to 1 MILE 4CM to 1KM

0	200	400	600	800 METRES	1
					KILOMETRES
					MILES
0	200	400	600 YARDS	½	

The present complex of buildings includes two of the finest medieval timbered barns in Europe, plus an Elizabethan Court Hall, early 17th-century farmhouse and an 18th-century

Waggon Lodge. There is also a walled garden and moats. Since 1987 it has been owned by Essex County Council.

Retrace your steps to the lane by the bridge over the river ⓓ and turn right to rejoin the shorter walk. At a public footpath sign, turn left along the enclosed, tarmac track to Fambridge

sign, turn right **F** on to a path by a hedge on the right and continue in a straight line across fields to emerge on to a lane in front of Cressing's medieval church. The church has a Norman nave and 13th-century chancel.

Turn left into Cressing, keep ahead past the village green along The Street and, at a public footpath sign where the road forks **G**, turn left along the left-hand edge of a field. Keep ahead into the next field but immediately turn right over a plank footbridge and continue along the right-hand field edge. In the corner, turn right over a stile and turn left, continuing initially by the left-hand field edge but bearing right and away from it to climb a stile. Keep along the left-hand edge of the next two fields, by a ditch on the left. Follow the ditch around a left-hand bend and cross a footbridge over it. Turn right, continuing between a fence on the left and the ditch on the right, and the path turns first left and then right. After crossing a footbridge into trees, turn left along an enclosed path, bear left on joining a track and go through a gate on to a road on the edge of Tye Green.

Turn right, cross Mill Lane and, at a public footpath sign, turn left **H** along an enclosed, tarmac track. Pass beside a vehicle scrapyard, keep ahead to climb a stile and continue across a field, making for a pylon where there is a waymarked post. Bear left to head across to the field corner, climb a stile, cross the railway line for the last time, climb another stile and head downhill along the left-hand field edge.

At the bottom, turn left along a fence-lined path, passing to the left of Bulford Mill, climb a stile and keep ahead to a lane. Turn left uphill and follow the lane around right- and left-hand bends to return to the starting point at Cressing Station.

Hall and turn left at a T-junction by the hall to continue along a gently descending track. Turn right along a track at an Essex Way post, pass under a railway bridge and the track winds across fields to a farm. Turn left here through a hedge gap and turn right to a road. Turn left and, at a public footpath

Epping Forest and Upshire

Start	High Beach, Epping Forest Centre, signposted from A121
Distance	9 miles (14.5km)
Approximate time	4½ hours
Parking	Epping Forest Centre
Refreshments	Pub and kiosk at start, pub at Bell Common, pub at Upshire
Ordnance Survey maps	Landranger 167 (Chelmsford, Harlow & Bishop's Stortford), Explorer 174 (Epping Forest & Lee Valley)

Approximately three-quarters of this walk is through the splendid woodlands at the northern end of Epping Forest, once part of the vast royal hunting-grounds of the Forest of Essex. At about the half-way point at Bell Common, you emerge from the forest and continue across more open country, enjoying extensive views, to the village of Upshire. You then plunge back into woodland for the final stretch. Route finding is generally easy except perhaps at the start, where you need to follow the directions carefully in order to reach the Green Ride, a clearly defined track through the forest.

During the Middle Ages, the Forest of Essex, subsequently known as Waltham Forest, covered much of the county, and its proximity to the capital made it one of the most popular of royal hunting-grounds. From the 17th century onwards, fellings and enclosures caused it to shrink rapidly and it became fragmented. The present Epping Forest is the largest of the remaining fragments, covering nearly 6,000 acres (2,428ha) and comprising mainly hornbeam, oak, beech and birch. It was fortunately saved from further destruction by the Corporation of the City of London. By an Act of Parliament in 1878, the Corporation became the Conservators of Epping Forest in order to preserve it 'as an open space for the recreation and enjoyment of the public'. In the 18th

century, Epping Forest was a favourite haunt of the notorious highwayman Dick Turpin.

Begin by taking the path between the Visitor Centre on the right and the Field Studies Centre on the left, heading across grass to the Field Studies building. Continue along a path that curves right by a small pool on the right and first ascend and then descend steps to go through a gate. Turn left alongside the boundary fence of the Epping Forest Centre and, at the fence corner, keep ahead to a T-junction. Turn left along a track and, just before it bears slightly left, turn right on to a path that descends to a road.

Cross over, keep ahead to a three-way junction and take the left-hand path, heading slightly uphill and then

Epping Forest

curving right to continue through the trees, keeping more or less in a straight line, to reach a sandy track in a clearing. Turn left along the track Ⓐ – this is the Green Ride – and, ignoring all side turns, follow it through the superb woodlands of Great Monk Wood to reach a road. Cross it and, passing to the right of a small car park, continue along the track opposite, descending and then rising to reach a T-junction. Turn left along a track to go through a car park on to a road.

Cross over, go through another car park, pass beside a barrier and take the broad track ahead. Keep on the main track all the time to pass to the right of the tree-covered earthworks of Ambresbury Banks, an Iron Age defence. Continue along an undulating track, which eventually passes beside a barrier to emerge from the forest and keeps ahead to a road Ⓑ. Turn left, and the road curves left to a T-junction at Bell Common. Turn left, in the Woodford direction, and at a public footpath sign, bear right on to an enclosed path Ⓒ.

The path bears right to a ladder-stile beside the M25. After climbing it, the right-of-way continues over the stile immediately in front and across a field, turning left down to the field edge and turning right along it. A slightly easier alternative is not to climb the second stile but bear left to continue along an enclosed path parallel to the motorway, turn right over a ladder-stile and walk along the left-hand field edge. Either way, bear left to climb a stile in the field corner and turn right along the right-hand edge of the next field, beside Griffin's Wood. At the corner of the wood, bear right through a gate and

SCALE 1:25000 or 2½ INCHES to 1 MILE 4CM to 1KM

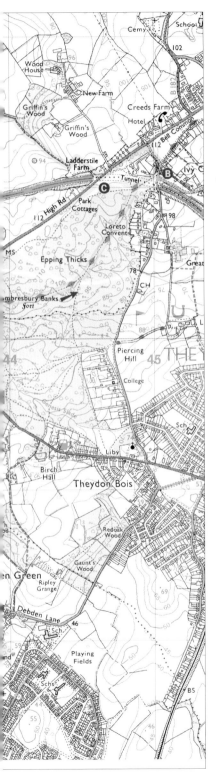

turn left along a tarmac drive. The drive heads gently uphill and curves left at the top to reach a crossroads.

Turn right, almost immediately turn left over a stile, at a public footpath sign to Lodge Farm, and walk diagonally across a field. On the far side pass through a hedge gap and cross a plank footbridge. Bear left to head across the corner of the next field to join a tarmac track at a bend and keep along the track to a T-junction just beyond a gate. Turn left to a lane **D**, turn left along the lane to a T-junction and turn left again to another T-junction.

Turn right into Upshire and, at a triangular green, bear left **E** along a track to a crossroads and public bridleway sign. If you wish to visit the church and pub, keep ahead a short distance along the road. Although the church looks traditional, with the usual Essex timber bell-turret, it was only built in 1902.

At the public bridleway sign turn left, go through a gate and walk along a track to cross the M25. Keep ahead uphill, follow the track around a left-hand bend and, at a fork, take the right-hand track, signposted Forest Way. After passing the imposing Woodredon House on the left, the track becomes a tarmac one and you continue along it, passing beside a gate and on through trees to a road **F**.

Turn left and almost immediately turn right along a winding track, at a public footpath sign to Loughton. Cross over the next road **G**, pass beside a barrier and continue along a track to emerge on to another road at a junction. Take the road ahead, which leads back to the King's Oak pub and the entrance to the Epping Forest Centre. ●

St Peter's Chapel, Bradwell Marshes and Tillingham

Start	Bradwell Marina at Bradwell Waterside
Distance	11 miles (17.5km)
Approximate time	5 hours
Parking	Bradwell Marina
Refreshments	Pub at Bradwell Waterside, pubs at Bradwell-on-Sea, pub at Tillingham
Ordnance Survey maps	Landranger 168 (Colchester, Halstead & Maldon), Explorer 176 (Blackwater Estuary)

Nowhere else in Essex do you experience the sense of remoteness and isolation as on this lengthy walk, much of which is across the lonely and desolate marshland of the Dengie Peninsula, which lies between the Blackwater and Crouch estuaries. Even the nuclear power station at Bradwell hardly intrudes on this otherwise unspoilt scene. Highlight of the walk is the isolated and tiny Saxon chapel of St Peter-on-the-Wall but the route also passes through three villages, two of which have medieval churches and all of which possess at least one pub.

Begin by facing the Blackwater estuary and take the paved path beside the Chandlery, which turns right and continues as a tarmac path. Descend steps, keep ahead to a road and turn right through the village of Bradwell Waterside. Where the road turns right, keep ahead along a path that passes in front of cottages, go through a barrier and bear slightly right across a field.

After going through a gap, continue across the next field and then along an enclosed path to emerge on to a road at a junction. Bear right along the road signposted to Bradwell Village and, at a public footpath sign, turn left over a stile **A**. Walk along a grassy path, keep ahead across a small field, go through a gap in the right-hand corner and

continue along the right-hand field edge. Keep ahead across the next field and, on the far side, cross a footbridge on to a track, turn right and follow the track to a lane **B**.

Turn left along the lane for about 1 mile (1.6km) to where it ends by Eastlands Farm. Keep ahead along a track, go through a gate and continue to the Saxon chapel of St Peter-on-the-Wall **C**.

This tiny and highly atmospheric church, situated amidst lonely marshes and overlooking the North Sea, was founded by St Cedd in the 7th century. It stands on the site of the 3rd-century Roman fort of Othona, and stones from the fort were used in its construction. In the later Middle Ages the population moved away to the village of Bradwell-on-Sea and the chapel became abandoned and redundant. For several centuries it was used as a barn but in 1920 it was restored and rededicated.

The track swings right in front of the chapel and, on reaching an embankment, head up on to it and turn right. You now continue along the top of this embankment above the wide and desolate Bradwell Marshes for the next 2 miles (3.2km), following it around a bulge – turning first left, then right (now closer to the sea), right again and left again. Where the embankment next turns left, bear right to descend from it and continue along a concrete track. At the next waymarked post, turn right Ⓓ along a track and, where it turns right

to a farm, keep ahead to climb two stiles. After climbing the second stile, walk across a field, keeping parallel to its right-hand edge, and make for a stile in the right-hand corner. Climb it, keep along the left-hand edge of the next field – above a ditch – follow the ditch first to the left and then to the right and continue across fields, bearing left to a waymarked post.

Turn right across a causeway between channels, keep ahead across two fields and, on the far side of the second field, bear left along a track. At a T-junction turn right, follow the track around a left-hand bend but almost immediately turn right, at a waymarked post, to cross a footbridge. Head diagonally across a field, go through a

The isolated and tiny Saxon chapel of St Peter-on-the-Wall

hedge gap to rejoin the previous track and continue along it towards a farm. After passing through the farm, keep ahead along a lane and, where it turns left, continue along the right-hand edge of a field.

Keep ahead at a crossroads – Tillingham church comes into view – and at the corner of the churchyard fence, turn left alongside it and turn right into the churchyard. Keeping to the left of the church, go through a kissing-gate on to a road and turn right ❸. Tillingham is a most appealing village, with weatherboarded cottages around a green presided over by the fine 12th- to 14th-century church.

Follow the road around right-, left- and right-hand bends and, just after another left bend, turn right ❺ along a narrow lane, signposted No Through Road. Keep along it to a farm, where you turn left to continue along a track. At a waymarked post, bear left through a spinney, cross a footbridge and keep ahead along a narrow path through trees and bushes to emerge into a field. The way now is straight ahead across the field to a stile.

Climb the stile, keep ahead through trees, climb another stile on the far side and continue across a field. After going through a hedge gap, walk along the right-hand edge of the next field to a lane ❻. Turn right and follow this winding lane into Bradwell-on-Sea. As its name indicates, the village was once on the coast but the sea has receded, leaving it nearly 2 miles (3.2km) inland. The 14th-century church has a west tower built of brick in 1706.

Keep ahead through the village, passing to the left of the church, to pick up the outward route and retrace your steps to the start. ●

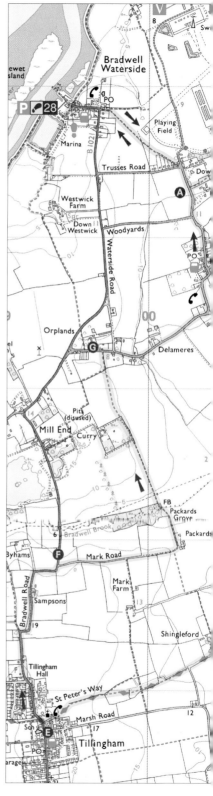

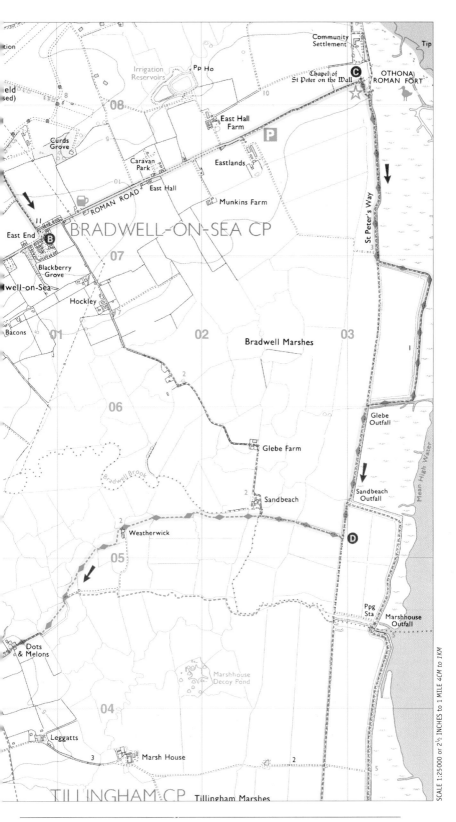

Further Information

 ## The National Trust

Anyone who likes visiting places of natural beauty and/or historic interest has cause to be grateful to the National Trust. Without it, many such places would probably have vanished by now.

It was in response to the pressures on the countryside posed by the relentless march of Victorian industrialisation that the trust was set up in 1895. Its founders, inspired by the common goals of protecting and conserving Britain's national heritage and widening public access to it, were Sir Robert Hunter, Octavia Hill and Canon Rawnsley: respectively a solicitor, a social reformer and a clergyman. The latter was particularly influential. As a canon of Carlisle Cathedral and vicar of Crosthwaite (near Keswick), he was concerned about threats to the Lake District and had already been active in protecting footpaths and promoting public access to open countryside. After the flooding of Thirlmere in 1879 to create a large reservoir, he became increasingly convinced that the only effective way to guarantee protection was outright ownership of land.

The purpose of the National Trust is to preserve areas of natural beauty and sites of historic interest by acquisition, holding them in trust for the nation and making them available for public access and enjoyment. Some of its properties have been acquired through purchase, but many of the Trust's properties have been donated. Nowadays it is not only one of the biggest landowners in the country, but also one of the most active conservation charities, protecting 581,113 acres (253,176 ha) of land, including 555 miles (892km) of coastline, and over 300 historic properties in England, Wales and Northern Ireland. (There is a separate National Trust for Scotland, which was set up in 1931.)

Furthermore, once a piece of land has come under National Trust ownership, it is difficult for its status to be altered. As a result of parliamentary legislation in 1907, the Trust was given the right to declare its property inalienable, so ensuring that in any subsequent dispute it can appeal directly to parliament.

As it works towards its dual aims of conserving areas of attractive countryside and encouraging greater public access (not easy to reconcile in this age of mass tourism), the Trust provides an excellent service for walkers by creating new concessionary paths and waymarked trails, maintaining stiles and foot bridges and combating the ever-increasing problem of footpath erosion.

For details of membership, contact the National Trust at the address on page 94.

 ## The Ramblers' Association

No organisation works more actively to protect and extend the rights and interests of walkers in the countryside than the Ramblers' Association. Its aims are clear: to foster a greater knowledge, love and care of the countryside; to assist in the protection and enhancement of public rights of way and areas of natural beauty; to work for greater public access to the countryside; and to encourage more people to take up rambling as a healthy, recreational leisure activity.

It was founded in 1935 when, following the setting up of a National Council of Ramblers' Federations in 1931, a number of federations earlier formed in London, Manchester, the Midlands and elsewhere came together to create a more effective pressure group, to deal with such problems as the disappearance and obstruction of footpaths, the prevention of access to open mountain and moorland and increasing hostility from landowners. This was the era of the mass trespasses, when there were sometimes violent

On the cliffs at The Naze

confrontations between ramblers and gamekeepers, especially on the moorlands of the Peak District.

Since then the Ramblers' Association has played an influential role in preserving and developing the national footpath network, supporting the creation of national parks and encouraging the designation and waymarking of long-distance routes.

Our freedom to walk in the countryside is precarious and requires constant vigilance. As well as the perennial problems of footpaths being illegally obstructed, disappearing through lack of use or extinguished by housing or road construction, new dangers can spring up at any time.

It is to meet such problems and dangers that the Ramblers' Association exists and represents the interests of all walkers. The address to write to for information on the Ramblers' Association and how to become a member is given on page 95.

Walkers and the Law

The average walker in a national park or other popular walking area, armed with the appropriate Ordnance Survey map, reinforced perhaps by a guidebook giving detailed walking instructions, is unlikely to run into legal difficulties, but it is useful to know something about the law relating to public rights of way. The right to walk over certain parts of the countryside has developed over a long period, and how such rights came into being is a complex subject, too lengthy to be discussed here. The following comments are intended simply as a helpful guide, backed up by the Countryside Access Charter, a concise summary of walkers' rights and obligations drawn up by the Countryside Agency (see page 92).

Basically there are two main kinds of public rights of way: footpaths (for walkers only) and bridleways (for walkers, riders on horseback and pedal cyclists). Footpaths and bridleways are shown by broken green lines on Ordnance Survey Pathfinder and Outdoor Leisure maps and broken red lines on Landranger maps. There is also a third category, called byways: chiefly broad tracks (green lanes) or farm roads, which walkers, riders and cyclists have to share, usually only occasionally, with motor vehicles. Many of these public paths have been in existence for hundreds of years and some even originated as prehistoric trackways

Countryside Access Charter

Your rights of way are:

- public footpaths – on foot only. Sometimes waymarked in yellow
- bridleways – on foot, horseback and pedal cycle. Sometimes waymarked in blue
- byways (usually old roads), most 'roads used as public paths' and, of course, public roads – all traffic has the right of way

Use maps, signs and waymarks to check rights of way. Ordnance Survey Pathfinder and Landranger maps show most public rights of way

On rights of way you can:

- take a pram, pushchair or wheelchair if practicable
- take a dog (on a lead or under close control)
- take a short route round an illegal obstruction or remove it sufficiently to get past

You have a right to go for recreation to:

- public parks and open spaces – on foot
- most commons near older towns and cities – on foot and sometimes on horseback
- private land where the owner has a formal agreement with the local authority

In addition you can use the following by local or established custom or consent, but ask for advice if you are unsure:

- many areas of open country, such as moorland, fell and coastal areas, especially those in the care of the National Trust, and some commons
- some woods and forests, especially those owned by the Forestry Commission
- country parks and picnic sites
- most beaches
- canal towpaths
- some private paths and tracks Consent sometimes extends to horse-riding and cycling

For your information:

- county councils and London boroughs maintain and record rights of way, and register commons
- obstructions, dangerous animals, harassment and misleading signs on rights of way are illegal and you should report them to the county council
- paths across fields can be ploughed, but must normally be reinstated within two weeks
- landowners can require you to leave land to which you have no right of access
- motor vehicles are normally permitted only on roads, byways and some 'roads used as public paths'

and have been in constant use for well over 2,000 years. Ways known as RUPPs (roads used as public paths) still appear on some maps. The legal definition of such byways is ambiguous and they are gradually being reclassified as footpaths, bridleways or byways.

The term 'right of way' means exactly what it says. It gives right of passage over what, in the vast majority of cases, is private land, and you are required to keep to the line of the path and not stray on to the land on either side. If you inadvertently wander off the right of way – either because of faulty map-reading or because the route is not clearly indicated on the ground – you are technically trespassing and the wisest course is to ask the nearest

available person (farmer or fellow walker) to direct you back to the correct route. There are stories about unpleasant confrontations between walkers and farmers at times, but in general most farmers are co-operative when responding to a genuine and polite request for assistance in route-finding.

Obstructions can sometimes be a problem and probably the most common of these is where a path across a field has been ploughed up. It is legal for a farmer to plough up a path provided that he restores it within two weeks, barring exceptionally bad weather. This does not always happen and here the walker is presented with a dilemma: to follow the line of the path, even if this inevitably means treading on crops, or to walk around the edge of the field. The latter course of action often seems the best but this means that you would be trespassing and not keeping to the exact line of the path. In the case of other obstructions which may block a path (illegal fences and locked gates etc), common sense has to be used in order to negotiate them by the easiest method – detour or removal. You should only ever remove as much as is necessary to get through, and if you can easily go round the obstruction without causing any damage, then you should do so. If you have any problems negotiating rights of way, you should report the matter to the rights of way department of the relevant council, which will take action with the landowner concerned.

Apart from rights of way enshrined by law, there are a number of other paths available to walkers. Permissive or concessionary paths have been created where a landowner has given permission for the public to use a particular route across his land. The main problem with these is that, as they have been granted as a concession, there is no legal right to use them and therefore they can be extinguished at any time. In practice, many of these concessionary routes have been established on land owned either by large public bodies such as the Forestry Commission, or by a private one, such as the National Trust, and as these mainly encourage walkers to use their paths, they are unlikely to be closed unless a change of ownership occurs.

Walkers also have free access to country parks (except where requested to keep away from certain areas for ecological reasons, e.g wildlife protection, woodland regeneration, etc), canal towpaths and most beaches. By custom, though not by right, you are generally free to walk across the open and uncultivated higher land of mountain, moorland and fell, but this varies from area to area and from one season to another – grouse moors, for example, will be out of bounds during the breeding and shooting seasons and some open areas are used as Ministry of Defence firing ranges, for which reason access will be restricted. In some areas the situation has been clarified as a result of 'access agreements' between the landowners and either the county council or the national park authority, which clearly define when and where you can walk over such open country.

Further Information

The wooden Saxon church at Greensted

Walking Safety

Although the reasonably gentle countryside that is the subject of this book offers no real dangers to walkers at any time of the year, it is still advisable to take sensible precautions and follow certain well-tried guidelines.

Always take with you both warm and waterproof clothing and sufficient food and drink. Wear suitable footwear, i.e. strong walking boots or shoes that give a good grip over stony ground, on slippery slopes and in muddy conditions. Try to obtain a local weather forecast and bear it in mind before you start. Do not be afraid to abandon your proposed route and return to your starting point in the event of a sudden and unexpected deterioration in the weather.

All the walks described in this book will be safe to do, given due care and respect, even during the winter. Indeed, a crisp, fine winter day often provides perfect walking conditions, with firm ground underfoot and a clarity unique to this time of the year. The most difficult hazard likely to be encountered is mud, especially when walking along woodland and field paths, farm tracks and

Blackmore church

bridleways – the latter in particular can often get churned up by cyclists and horses. In summer, an additional difficulty may be narrow and overgrown paths, particularly along the edges of cultivated fields. Neither should constitute a major problem provided that the appropriate footwear is worn.

Useful Organisations

Council for the Protection of Rural England
25 Buckingham Palace Road,
London SW1W 0PP.
Tel. 020 7976 6433

Countryside Agency
John Dower House,
Crescent Place, Cheltenham,
Gloucestershire GL50 3RA.
Tel. 01242 521381

Essex County Council
County Hall, Market Road,
Chelmsford, Essex CM1 1QH.
Tel. 01245 437132

Essex Wildlife Trust
Fingringhoe Wick Nature Reserve,
South Green Road, Fingringhoe,
Colchester, Essex CO5 7DN.
Tel. 01206 729678

Forestry Commission
Information Branch,
231 Corstorphine Road,
Edinburgh EH12 7AT. Tel. 0131 334 0303

Long Distance Walkers' Association
21 Upcroft, Windsor, Berkshire SL4 3NH.
Tel. 01753 866685

National Trust
Membership and general enquiries:
PO Box 39, Bromley, Kent BR1 3XL.
Tel. 020 8315 1111
East Anglia Regional Office:
Blickling Hall, Blickling,
Norwich NR11 6NF. Tel. 01263 733471

Ordnance Survey
Romsey Road, Maybush,
Southampton SO16 4GU.
Tel. 08456 05 05 05 (Lo-call)

Cottages at Pleshey

Ramblers' Association
2nd Floor, Camelford House, 87–90 Albert
Embankment, London SE1 7TW.
Tel. 020 7339 8500

Tourist information:
East of England Tourist Board,
Toppesfield Hall, Hadleigh,
Suffolk IP7 7DN.
Tel. 01473 822922
Essex Tourist Information Centre
County Hall, Market Road,
Chelmsford, Essex CM1 1GG.
Tel. 01245 283400
Fax 01245 430705
Local tourist information offices:
Braintree: 01376 550066
Chelmsford: 01245 283400
Clacton: 01255 423400
Colchester: 01206 282920
Harwich: 01255 506139
Maldon: 01653 600048
Redbridge/Ilford: 020 8478 3020
Saffron Walden: 01799 510444
Southend-on-Sea: 01702 215120
Thurrock: 01708 863733
Waltham Abbey: 01992 652295

Youth Hostels Association
Trevelyan House,
8 St Stephen's Hill,
St Albans, Hertfordshire AL1 2DY.
Tel. 01727 855215

 *Ordnance Survey
Maps of Essex*
The area of Essex is covered by Ordnance
Survey 1:50 000 scale (2cm to 1km or
$1^{1}/_{4}$ inches to 1 mile) Landranger map
sheets 154, 155, 166, 167, 168, 169, 177,
178. These all-purpose maps are packed
with information to help you explore the
area and show viewpoints, picnic sites,
places of interest and caravan and
camping sites.

To examine the Essex area in more
detail, and especially if you are planning
walks, Ordnance Survey Explorer maps at
1:25 000 scale (4cm to 1km or $2^{1}/_{2}$ inches
to 1 mile) scale are ideal. Maps covering
this area are:

174 Epping Forest & Lee Valley
175 Southend-on-Sea & Basildon
176 Blackwater Estuary, Maldon
183 Chelmsford & The Rodings
184 Colchester, Harwich & Clacton-on-Sea
195 Braintree & Saffron Walden
196 Sudbury, Hadleigh & Dedham Vale

To get to Essex use the Ordnance
Survey Great Britain Routeplanner Map 1
at 1:625 000 scale (1cm to 6.25 km or 1
inch to 10 miles) and Travelmaster map 9
South-East England at 1:250 000 scale
(1cm to 2.5km or 1 inch to 4 miles).
Ordnance Survey maps and guides are
available from most booksellers, stationers
and newsagents.

Index

Entries in *italic type* refer to illustrations